"This book offers much-needed encouragement to families who are tired of hearing society's endless whine about the impossibility of mothers staying home to raise their own children. The fact is, it can be done, and it is being done, with ingenuity and good cheer. . . . Her Eleven Miserly Guidelines are completely practical, and at the top of the list is the most important: 'Don't confuse frugality with depriving yourself.' "

— Ginny Silva
In a review for *Christian Parenting Today*

"Jonni McCoy shows great understanding in the power of living frugally. It can be done, and she can show you how, so if you want to take back control of your finances, start here."

— Pat Veretto
Frugal Living Guide at *About.com*

"Let Jonni McCoy be your guide through the jungle of hidden costs, misleading purchasing assumptions, and costly habits. She leads you out of the murky water of living up to the unrealistic standards of our society and into the calmness of balanced checkbooks and a peaceable home life."

— Jill Bond
author of *Dinner's in the Freezer!*

"In this day of two-income families, *Miserly Moms* offers a refreshing look into the possibilities of having a stay-at-home parent. Today's families *can* live a full and joyful life, even on limited means. With warmth, humor, and candor, McCoy shows us how!"

— Deborah Taylor-Hough
author of *Frozen Assets: How to Cook for a Day and Eat for a Month*

"Practical financial advice that makes sense, is easy to follow, and can be implemented today. One-income families especially will benefit from Jonni McCoy's money-saving insights."

— Cheryl Gochnauer
author of *So You Want to Be a Stay-at-Home Mom*

Miserly MOMS

JONNI McCOY

Miserly
MOMS

Living Well on Less in a
Tough Economy

BETHANYHOUSE
MINNEAPOLIS, MINNESOTA

Miserly Moms
Fourth Edition
Copyright © 1994, 1996, 2001, 2009
by Jonni McCoy

Miserly Moms is a trademark and servicemark of Jonni McCoy.

Cover design by Dan Pitts

Scripture quotations are from the New King James Version of the Bible. Copyright ©
1979, 1980, 1982 by Thomas Nelson, Inc. Used by permission. All rights reserved.

Published by Bethany House Publishers
11400 Hampshire Avenue South
Bloomington, Minnesota 55438

Printed in the United States of America

Library of Congress Cataloging-in-Publication Data

McCoy, Jonni.
    Miserly Moms : living well on less in a tough economy / Jonni McCoy. — 4th ed.
        p. cm.
    Included bibliographical references and index.
    Summary: "Practical, proven strategies and tips to help families live more fru-
gally without being deprived, while still reaching their financial goals"—Provided
by publisher.
    ISBN 978-0-7642-0641-2 (pbk. : alk. paper) 1. Consumer education. 2. Home
economics—Accounting I. Title.

    TX335.M384   2009
    640.73—dc22
                                                                        2009005552

ABOUT THE AUTHOR

JONNI MCCOY holds a Bachelor of Arts degree in Speech Communication from the University of California at Santa Barbara. Prior to motherhood, she spent ten years as a senior buyer and supervisor for electronics firms such as Apple Computer and National Semiconductor. She presents seminars on living for less to women's groups and other conferences. She has been practicing her frugal ways since 1991. Jonni has appeared on *The Gayle King Show* and *The 700 Club,* and radio programs such as *FamilyLife Today* and the *Dick Staub Show.* She has also been featured in *Good Housekeeping, Family Circle, Family Fun, Working Mother,* and *Woman's Day* magazines. Jonni and her husband, Beau, make their home in Colorado Springs, Colorado, where they homeschool their children.

For more help with saving money, visit our Web site.

We offer numerous resources for the frugal person (or frugal wannabe).

There are articles, links to other money-saving sites, and much more! Drop by soon!

WWW.MISERLYMOMS.COM

*I would like to dedicate this book
to my husband, Beau,
and to my children, Jeremy and Jessica.
They never failed in their belief in me.*

CONTENTS

Why This Book Is Different

When I first wrote this book, our family lived in one of the most expensive parts of America—the San Francisco Bay Area. Most families were spending half their income to pay the high rent or mortgage. Consequently, most families needed both parents to work just to get by. We were one of those families. According to statistics, my husband and I were a middle-income family, with my job providing half of our joint income. I was a career woman who received much joy from her work.

After our first child was born, I began to feel God tugging at my heart to stay home to raise our family. At first I thought I hadn't heard correctly. We couldn't live in the Bay Area on half of our joint income. At least that's what we believed. Trying to interpret what God was saying to me, I arranged a job-sharing program where I worked part time. We continued in that lifestyle for several years. Once it became clear that the part-time arrangement was not God's plan, and that I was supposed to stay home full time, we were back to square one.

We thought we would have to move to a less expensive community in order to live on my husband's salary alone. So that's what we decided to do, but things changed at the last minute. We made an offer on a house, and someone made an offer on our home. One night I realized that I didn't want my husband commuting several hours each day, and I didn't like the idea of being so far away from our church and our friends. We were able to get out of both house offers with no penalties. But I had already quit my job. So there we were, living on half of our income in an expensive area.

Our choices were either for me to go back to work or to somehow reduce our expenses. But I knew I was supposed to stay at home with my family, so instead of bringing in a salary, I began to research how we could make our money go further. This opened my eyes to the hidden costs in the way we lived, and I questioned whether some people could even afford to be working!

When we calculated what our loss of income would do to our budget, we didn't realize how many hidden costs would disappear once I stopped working. Given the cost of child care, taxes, gasoline, parking, convenience foods (we were often too tired to cook after work), lunches out, office clothes, and all the other amenities associated with working, not much of our salaries were even used at home. I wasn't alone in this realization. I read that some financial experts had calculated the cost of working as nine to twenty-five dollars per hour. I was stunned! This meant that many of us who worked were actually paying for the privilege of working. I was inspired by the challenge of reducing our budget instead of increasing our salary.

This book is not about how to make money at home. Many other books have done a fine job of that. I've listed a few of these books in "Additional Resources," appendix B, for those interested in pursuing this option.

Many books have been written on how to be thrifty. Some are theoretical in their approach, filled with interviews with other frugal people and impersonal statistics. Some are focused on a specific way to save, such as reducing credit-card debt or using grocery coupons. Others try to be broad but are too extreme, cutting back in every aspect of life, whether it is cost-effective or not.

There is nothing theoretical in this book. It is a testimony of our journey. We were a two-income yuppie family that chose to make a lifestyle change. We have lived out all of the advice I suggest here.

I look at saving money as a means to an end. It is a job I perform in order to afford my staying at home. I don't do the things that I share in this book just for fun. I enjoy my luxuries if and when I can afford them. Some people take pleasure in being frugal as a hobby. I, however, must be convinced of the savings return before I do something frugal. For example, I find little profit in reusing envelopes or dryer lint. Those activities may save a penny or two, but that would not be a good use of my time. If you only have a little time to invest in saving, it might as well be put to use in the most effective places. Frugal people are looking for the best overall value. That value may not be money. Cheap people always put money first.

I believe in putting your efforts to work where they will save you the most. That is why the book is organized as it is—from the greatest savings opportunities to the least. Groceries are the first and largest topic that I discuss because it is where most families can save the most. We were able to save hundreds of dollars per month in this category alone.

I discuss other areas where we also achieved significant savings. When added together with the elimination of working expenses (the cost of working), we made a large dent in what we spent—the savings adding up to what some people might earn at a job.

Some people already have thought of the ideas in this book, especially those with parents or grandparents who lived through the Depression. Those people knew how to make what was necessary and live without the unnecessary. Their wisdom has been lost, and many think we shouldn't have to live without the things we desire. But others have asked for help with creative ideas to cut costs in their lives. It is for these people that I wrote this book. My desire is to get their creative juices in motion so they can start thinking of ways to save and meet their goals.

Your spouse doesn't have to earn a high wage in order for you to live on one income. I know several families (including my own) who have willingly lived on less than half of what the average family in their area earns.

We have added another member to our family. We have pets. We go on vacations. We even buy nice things for our kids and for ourselves.

These money-saving principles really can make a difference.

What do you have to lose?

If I Can Do It, You Can Do It

You might think that it comes naturally for me to be organized and self-disciplined and to spend extra time shopping and baking. This isn't true. It doesn't come naturally for me. I share my background not out of vanity but to show you that anyone can learn to live frugally.

The first thing you should know is that I am not "tight." It is not in my nature. I do what I have to in order to reach a goal. I can (and do) return to my luxuries in a snap when I can afford them. Some people are frugal because they have never known any other way. Others enjoy being frugal even though they can afford not to be. I knew what the "good life" was, but I was able to learn to live frugally when it was necessary to do so.

Until the age of eight, I lived in a northern California suburb, Walnut Creek. My family lived an average middle-class life with a three-bedroom house, a dog, and simple vacations to Yosemite and the beach. Then life changed radically. My dad accepted a job with an American organization in Pakistan, and later we all moved to Nigeria. When the plane landed overseas, our life was never the same. We suddenly had five servants and a three-story house with bedrooms the size of most living rooms. All of our chores were done for us. I never had to clean my room or make my bed (I still don't make my bed). We even had coffee (or cocoa) brought to our rooms to awaken us in the morning. We traveled around the world several times in the six years that we lived overseas. We returned to the United States when I was fifteen, buying a three-bedroom house in Silicon Valley (south of San Francisco).

I share this to help you understand that I knew what good things were, but I have been able to learn to do without them. I was used to the convenience of having meals made and work done for me by others, so learning to apply myself to the art of being thrifty was new to me. The skills that I have acquired and share in this book were necessary to reach my financial goal of staying at home with my kids. It didn't all come to me at once. I started with one idea, then added another once the first one became second nature. Eventually I started to see a difference. Even if you only apply one or two ideas from this book, you will help your budget.

So if I can do it, you can do it!

CHAPTER 1

Coming-Home Stories

WHAT SOME MOMS SAY ABOUT THEIR DECISION

Taking the plunge and quitting your job is a scary step. It's riddled with consequences and fears. Will we have enough money? Am I doing the right thing?

Most women I talk to are glad they quit. Many reveal their fears were unfounded, and that things were not as hard as they expected. Almost all report seeing benefits in their children and in themselves since being at home.

Coming home can bring a calm to the family: a peaceful stability rather than a rushed schedule, and the kids can rely on a parent to be there when they need her. There is nothing more devastating to a child than being told he can't come home even though he doesn't feel well because Mom doesn't have any more time off. The rewards of a job are fleeting compared to the rewards of raising and shaping a future adult. But I don't want you to take only my word for it.

I get letters weekly from women who share their stories of the transition from working mom to at-home mom or mostly-at-home mom. They are heartening to anyone fearing the changes coming home might bring. Following are a few excerpts from these letters to encourage you. For more of these stories, please visit my Web site at *www.miserly moms.com*.

For more on the subject of coming home, please read the books listed at the end of this chapter.

SHELLY OF VIRGINIA

Deciding to quit work to be at home with my children at the age of thirty-five was no easy decision. I had worked all my adult life. It's been over a year since I came home to be with my children, and I wouldn't trade it for the world. I had always said that I could never stay at home with the kids, that I was a working kind of girl and that's the way it was. God in my life changed all that, and so did my three great kids. I do child care in my home, trying to help other moms who think they have to work as well. I am always encouraging them to cut costs so they can come home to be with their own kids, as I have. The extra money I make in providing child care pays the groceries and another bill or two, so it's a financial help to say the least.

I strongly encourage any women who have the least bit of desire to quit work and come home to look at every avenue, because, trust me, all the money in the world can't buy your happiness. One expense I cut without realizing it was medical costs. It's amazing how when you don't have that kind of stress in your life, and your kids aren't exposed to everyone else's sicknesses, you don't have to visit the doctor so often and spend your money there and at the drugstore. That's a big savings in itself. Where there's a will, there's a way, and believe me, it's worth it in the long run. You'll never regret it!

KATE OF PENNSYLVANIA

At first my husband didn't get it. He anticipated dual incomes and all the things that could be done with that money. I have had to work on his thinking a lot to get him to see that there is no bigger payoff than a happy home and happy children. I never have to worry about coordinating schedules or who will watch my kids when they get sick. We aren't rich financially, but we are spiritually.

DONNA OF NEW YORK

When my husband and I were first married, we had quite a bit of debt. We were paying off our debt and thinking we were on the right track, but then things changed. We had our first baby, and I left my stressful job to work part time in a grant-funded position.

And then we bought a house.

And then we got pregnant again.

And then our car died.

And then the roof caved in.

And then my grant-funded position was cut.

And then I started to cry.

After the crying, getting hit unexpectedly with other hard and heavy bills, and being in lots more debt, I started to wise up. This reality check made me realize how unfrugal I was. My dear husband, who loved to spend money (before we were married he ate out every night and didn't even know you could pay more than a minimum monthly payment on a bill!), was very supportive in my endeavor. I started reading the experts (*Miserly Moms* and *Tightwad Gazette*, among others) and got into a positive frame of mind—that this was the best thing to do. Once I felt proactive and money-smart rather than desperate and "cheap," I realized my life had changed for the better. I started cooking almost everything from scratch, grocery shopping at different stores, mending clothes, shopping at Salvation Army, and finding lots of free family stuff to do.

Now we are down to one last debt, and it's steadily going down—any extra money we get goes toward it. We still love to go away, but now our trips involve driving and staying with family or at hostels, and finding free stuff to do while bringing our food along. My wonderful husband and I are so proud of what we are doing to make our lives better. We are not materialistically wealthy—our wealth and riches are much, much greater than that.

CINDY OF NORTH CAROLINA

My husband and I have been married for fourteen years and have three children. For most of that time, I was working full time as a newspaper copy editor. Because we worked opposite shifts, child care wasn't an issue—but we didn't see much of each other! When my third child was a year old, we decided I could come home. Two months after coming home, that son was diagnosed with spinal muscular atrophy, which meant wheelchairs, ramps, ventilators, physical therapy, doctors, more doctors . . . and the list goes on. Though our insurance was good, it wasn't *that* good. So back to work I went.

Three years and piles of medical bills later, another son was diagnosed with Tourette's syndrome and learning disabilities. More bills. More stress. Lots more tears. Our marriage was rocky, I was unhappy, my husband was unhappy, the kids were unhappy. Nothing was getting done well. We decided I should try coming home again. This time I prepared. We cashed in investments to pay off a car loan and other debts, and cancelled all the extras—cable TV, cell phone, etc. I switched from the convenient, swanky grocery store to the one with no perks and immediately saved twenty-five dollars a week. We stopped going out to eat every Sunday after church, saving more than a hundred dollars a month. I stopped going to the bagel shop every morning, saving ten dollars a week. Funny thing is, after cutting out the little things, we had just as much at the end of the paycheck as we had when we were both working!

It's been nine months since I left my job, and I doubt I'll ever go back. The amount of stress that walked out the door when I came home has been astounding. I'm not always hurrying the kids because I have to get ready for work. My husband isn't stressed about hurrying home so I can go to work. We don't have to worry about sudden changes in one of the schedules. The kids are more relaxed. We're more relaxed.

Money is still tight, and because of our children's medical needs, it probably always will be. Even the children understand the benefits. I often hear them say how glad they are that they get to come home after school and don't have to go to child care. Many of my daughter's friends come home to an empty house. Mine are all glad they get to enjoy a real summer vacation—no rushing to child care or day camps, etc. And they do understand that the cost of their *not* going to child care means fewer material things. Their cousin has all the latest toys and lives in a huge house—but she is not home to enjoy them. My kids actually *get it*! It's been a long journey home, but worth every minute!

ELLEN OF OKLAHOMA

I was a successful paralegal with a promising career in a fantastic firm. My husband and I both worked long, hard hours and had a nice home, two cars, and plenty of extras. Then I got pregnant. I wanted to stay at home as my mother had, but we just couldn't make the math work out. We had decided that I would try working full time, but part of the time in the office and part of the time telecommuting from home.

Then, five days after our daughter was born, my husband looked at me and said, "Whatever it takes, you're not going back to work." How I had prayed for his cooperation in this effort.

We slashed our budget. Took out all the extras. Stopped eating out, no cell phone, no impulse shopping. I shop nice, quality resale stores for clothes for all of us. It's amazing what you can do when you get creative and determined to make it all work out! Our food bill is a constant challenge to me to find new and cheaper options. *Miserly Moms* has recently given me new incentive to get devoted to budget cutting again. And I am so glad I'm the one raising my daughter—not an endless rotation of child-care workers. In the beginning we were afraid to even try. Now with an eighteen-month-old daughter, we can't imagine living any other way.

ANNE OF PENNSYLVANIA

I fully expected that the first six months would be painful and that I'd feel some regret about our decision. It's been six months now, and what I find instead is that this was the best decision for our family, and we are all reaping the rewards. Life is sane again, our kids are happy, the finances are manageable, and my stress level is low. Do I miss work? Nope. After years of high-level stress, it is the greatest relief to let all of that go. I have the mental energy to manage our home, finances, and lifestyle, which is challenge enough! I am happy with the lifestyle we now have, and despite several enticing opportunities to return to work, I remain steadfast in my commitment. It has all been worth the pain of self-examination and change. Do I recommend it for other families? You betcha!

LISA OF CALIFORNIA

Most people know that military pay is not elaborate, but my husband and I had always agreed about the importance of my being home with our children, for which I am most thankful. Prior to our marriage I had worked as a secretary/administrative assistant, but knew in my heart it was not something I wanted to continue once I was a mom. At that time we made less than $17,000 a year, yet I don't have any memories whatsoever of feeling bad about my decision to come home. Through any financial challenge, I truly believe God blessed our choice. We always had enough food, our bills were paid, and I was able to be with my daughter.

The interesting thing about staying home is that while many people can manage it, too many think they can't. I believe it all comes down to how willing/unwilling you are to slash expenses in your life and take the time to make these changes.

These days I am a mom-at-home who also has health challenges. I still would not have it any other way. My job here is being the "home manager." I don't get paid for it, but I get great satisfaction knowing that I am making my husband's salary stretch as far as possible, and that we are still able to live as we originally intended. I see too many couple friends of ours struggling to work, get child care for their kids, commute, get supper on the table, and get everything else done they need to accomplish before the next day—only to start all over again!

And do you know what? Most of them are not any better off than we are.

TERRI OF TEXAS

I was a marine biologist working for the government, and had several published papers. I shopped whenever I wanted to and bought just about whatever I wanted. My dear husband and I would go out to eat several times a week.

When I was pregnant, we had looked at several child care centers we liked and picked one. But after the baby came, I knew I could not find it in my heart to go back to work. My husband said it would be okay for me to stay home as long as we could pay the bills. Now he wouldn't have it any other way, nor would I!

I am learning to cook, sew, raise animals, and enjoy the simple things in life! This has been the best decision I have made in my life as well as in the lives of my children. No one can take the place of a loving mother (or father) who stays home with the children. Material goods are nothing compared to the life and upbringing of a child. This time is so important to them. Don't cheat them out of time with you because of material things you "think" you need!

CHARLOTTE OF MASSACHUSETTS

We are a family of six, and I haven't worked since 1992. I am proud of myself and my husband for achieving this. I miss the indulgences of having extra money on hand, but when I stop to think about the blessings we possess, I am *so* grateful.

When one is surrounded by a wealthy (and therefore

luxurious) community, it is easy to become whiny, which saps the strength and the joy out of life.

KELLY OF OREGON

Having been on both sides of the fence, I wholeheartedly agree that there are actually very few families that absolutely need to have both parents working. When at all possible, I strongly believe that one parent should be at home for the kids. More and more families are making this decision, and I would not be surprised to see more one-income families than two-income families in the near future.

TRACY OF ARIZONA

I spent all of my twenties working in offices, taking classes, and trying to make a career. I thought true satisfaction came through being successful in business (back in my feminazi days). But for all my hard work, I realized that after twelve years of devoting my life to a career, I had gotten nowhere great. I was making decent money but nothing spectacular. What I noticed mostly was that I was really dissatisfied being a slave to a company.

Coming home has been one of the most important steps I've taken in my life. I now have a baby daughter, and I can't even imagine putting her in child care or with a baby-sitter all day. To me, being home and being a mother is the best job I've ever had!

Resources

Home by Choice: Raising Emotionally Secure Children in an Insecure World, Brenda Hunter (Multnomah Books, 2006).

My Heart's at Home: Becoming the Intentional Mom Your Family Needs, Jill Savage Clarkson (Harvest House Publishers, 2007).

The Power of Mother Love, Brenda Hunter (WaterBrook Press, 1999).

So You Want to Be a Stay-at-Home Mom, Cheryl Gochnauer (Inter-Varsity Press, 1999).

Staying Home: From Full-Time Professional to Full-Time Parent, Darcie Sanders and Martha Bullen (Spencer & Waters, 2001).

CHAPTER 2

The Eleven Miserly Guidelines

The art of being miserly interested me when I needed to find a creative alternative to working. When I quit my job, we had planned to move to a less expensive area. Then shortly after deciding not to move, I became pregnant again. Having already decided to stay home with our first child instead of returning to work, that door was now firmly shut (who's going to hire a pregnant woman?). Since I was not going to bring in money by working, I decided to attack the problem from the other side—by reducing the amount of money that went out of the house.

The first thing I did was to identify those items in our budget that were not fixed. That included any expense that fluctuated (such as food, gasoline, clothes, utilities). My next plan was to chip away at these expenses. I started with the highest bill—groceries. The Eleven Miserly Guidelines were originally notes that I kept in a binder for myself for reducing my grocery bill—the highest expense after our mortgage. I never intended to share the guidelines with anyone. But friends kept borrowing my notes, wanting to learn how to save money. With the encouragement of friends, I wrote some articles, then the first edition of *Miserly Moms*. As I learned more and expanded my horizons beyond the grocery store, I added more notes to my notebook. Even though the Eleven Miserly Guidelines pertain mainly to food, the general principles can be applied to other areas of your household.

By doing some rethinking on how I shopped and cooked, I immediately lowered our food bill from a hundred dollars to sixty-five dollars per week (this was 1991). That was a savings of $140 the first month. As I learned more ways to save and applied them, I spent less money. These ways to save eventually became my eleven guidelines. I was able to lower our food bill to forty dollars per week on many occasions. This total included household needs such as paper towels, toilet paper, shampoo, diapers, etc. The forty-dollar weekly total was not achieved every week; many weeks we spent sixty-five dollars. Your goal, of course, can only happen if all eleven guidelines are being applied faithfully.

If I compare this savings to the value of a part-time job, my budget cuts have proved to be more profitable. An average twenty-hour-per-week job (less taxes, baby-sitting, and other expenses) would provide only one dollar per hour profit. I "earned" more than that by applying my guidelines. If you believe these ideas may be too much work for you, divide what you have saved on groceries in a week by the hours spent doing the shopping and cooking. It should reveal a decent savings— tax-free and at a minimal cost (more on that in chapter 6, "Don't Buy Everything at the Same Store").

When I updated this book in 2009, I noticed that the cost of most groceries had tripled—some went up fivefold. The cost of heating and gasoline had also tripled. But our income has not increased by that same percentage. The cost of keeping our lifestyles is getting higher and tougher to maintain. These tips that I share are in an effort to keep your lifestyle intact as much as possible. Shopping and cooking differently can make a huge impact in that quest.

I have found many helpful resources to reduce our budget shortage. The most helpful have been cookbooks that contain recipes on how to make things yourself—cereals, jams, etc. The ones written in the late 1800s to the 1930s are my favorites. They are full of recipes for homemade versions of things that we think can only be purchased ready-made. Some of my favorites are listed at the end of chapter 8, "Make Your Own Whenever Possible."

With ideas gleaned from these "classics," I have formed some guidelines for grocery buying that make significant savings possible. In the following chapters, I have outlined the general guidelines along with some specific suggestions.

Some of these ideas may be a stretch for some people and basic to others; take what you like and leave the rest. For those just starting out on the odyssey of reduced spending, all eleven ideas may be overwhelming. After I spoke at a seminar, a woman came up to me in distress. She thought she had to apply all eleven ideas immediately. As I told her, take one step at a time. When it becomes comfortable, apply another guideline. Even if you only choose to try a few of the ideas, you will save. The more ideas you follow, the greater the savings.

THE ELEVEN MISERLY GUIDELINES

1. Don't confuse frugality with depriving yourself.
2. Remove little wasters of your money.
3. Keep track of food prices.
4. Don't buy everything at the same store.
5. Buy in bulk whenever possible.
6. Make your own whenever possible.

7. Eliminate convenience foods.

8. Cut back on meats.

9. Waste nothing.

10. Institute a soup-and-bread night or baked-potato night.

11. Cook several meals at once and freeze them.

GUIDELINE 1:

Don't Confuse Frugality With Depriving Yourself

This is the most important aspect of being successful at saving money. If I think I am being cheap when I try to save money, I will never stick to my guidelines. My underlying goal of staying at home is more important than any guideline I try to follow. It is essential to my success.

When I first started my frugal lifestyle, I feared what it would involve. I believed that frugal people lived undesirable lives: wearing stained and torn clothing or reusing plastic wrap. I refused to participate in any of that. But such a definition of a frugal lifestyle does not have to be yours. There are many degrees of frugal lifestyles. I was determined to maintain a sense of class and still be frugal.

If any money-saving activity makes you feel cheap or tight, you will eventually abandon your efforts. That is not the price we need to pay to reach our goals. I don't need to feel tight and cheap in order to stay home with my kids. There are ways to save money *and* keep my dignity. Unfortunately, many people think the two cannot be connected. You can be frugal and generous; you can be frugal and classy; and sadly, you can be wealthy and stingy.

GOAL SETTING

As I have stated, I am not tight by nature. And I believe that one can maintain a sense of class while being frugal. I know many people who love to be thrifty, but not because they need to be. Rather, it is a hobby or an obsession with them. Many frugal newsletters advocate Dumpster diving and reusing envelopes and dryer lint. I always have to ask myself, *Are these things really worth my time? What do they pay me in terms of reaching my goals?* A reused envelope saves you a penny. Dumpster diving may turn up things you can use, but did you need those things in the first place? Even if you did, what toxic elements were you exposed to in order to save a few dollars?

While I was working, many women I knew wanted to be at home with their kids, but most believed the price of staying home would be too high. These were career women who were used to good clothes, nice vacations, eating out regularly, and extra cash for impulse buying. They believed that in order to live without their income, they would have to resort to a cheap and undesirable lifestyle. So most remained working. I am living proof that there is a balance between these two.

In order to make any of the ideas in this book work for you, you must be very clear about why you are making the changes. Keep your goal at the forefront of your mind. Write it down and put it in an obvious place if you need the reminder. Next to the written goal, put a picture of something that helps to remind you of that goal. Without a clear goal or reason for change, you will abandon it quickly. My goal for staying home

---

FRUGAL ≠ STINGY

Do not eat the bread of a miser, nor desire his delicacies; for as he thinks in his heart, so is he.

Proverbs 23:6–7

---

was to be home for my children. I put a picture of them on my fridge, my bathroom mirror, and my car visor. If I ever got frustrated having to do without, I looked at the picture and remembered why I chose to do this. We still go on vacations, but they're less extravagant ones. We still eat out, but less often. I remind myself that the temporary luxury of a prepackaged meal, a shopping spree, or a meal out is less important than reaching my goal. And it doesn't take very much time.

All of the following guidelines are tools for reaching the goal you have written down. Some will be harder to follow than others. Just remember that all of the changes you make are for a good reason—reaching your ultimate goal. You might need to start thinking about your desires in terms of *needs vs. wants*. Some things you think are necessary may actually be *wants* and could be exchanged for more money toward real needs. Some things you spend money on may have to wait. Our society tells us that we should have what we want *now*. That's not reality. We need to revisit the thinking of our elders who knew the virtue of saving up for things and doing without until they could afford them.

Money and class are not synonymous. We can be classy and thrifty at the same time. I'm not saying that it's always easy. I enjoy nice things and going somewhere on impulse. Always planning for everything is hard. That's why we need to have a written reminder of our goal and some incentive boosters to help when we feel uninspired. Here are two of my favorite incentive boosters:

Track your success. Divide the savings of one week by the hours spent saving it (shopping, cooking, etc.). Calculate the amount "earned" per hour. For example, last week I saved $60, and it took me seven hours to do it (planning, shopping, cooking from scratch). That means I made $8.50 profit per hour—tax-free, no sitters, negligible expenses.

Have a visual reminder. Put the budgeted grocery money in an envelope. You can see the leftover money when the week is over. That's yours to spend however you wish.

Hanging on to your reasons for being frugal will make the rest of the guidelines easier to hang on to as well. If you find your new frugal changes difficult to adjust to, remember that it's not our circumstances that define our life but how we view our circumstances.

CHAPTER 4

GUIDELINE 2:

Remove Little Wasters of Your Money

When I kept track of everything I spent over a month's time, I was surprised at how many times I had squandered money. Going over receipts is an activity that I recommend to anyone who is serious about saving money.

Those frequent trips to department stores and fast-food lunches will keep you from reaching your financial goals. It is amazing how much of a drain they are on the budget. When I feel like dropping in for an unplanned shopping or munchies spree, I remind myself that those trips make things unattainable that are a higher priority on my list. Those trivial buys here and there can wipe out all that you have saved. One lunch per week at a fast-food restaurant costs twenty dollars per month per person. That number changes to sixty dollars per month if my kids and I eat lunch out once per week. I could apply that toward a bill or our vacation fund.

I have friends who say they "need" to shop for recreation, and work full time to pay for it. I wonder if the recreation is to ease the stress of work or the work is to pay for the recreation. In either case, the drains need to be plugged if any progress is to be made in reaching financial goals.

We must reprogram our thinking about money. It should never be used to make ourselves feel good or to be a measure of someone's love for us. Money should be looked at as a tool. It's there to get you where you need to go. And if you don't have a plan for it, it will be wasted. A budget is a plan for our money much like a date book is a plan for our time.

BUDGETING

In order to meet my goals, I have to make a budget and stick to it. Anything I want to do that isn't budgeted has to wait until I save enough for it. The importance of a budget cannot be overstated. It is your tool to making everything work. If the word *budget* gives you the shivers, replace the word with *plan*. That's all a budget is—a plan for your money.

The first step in budgeting is to see where your money is going. Make a list of all the expenses you have every month. If you have a computer, get a software program that will keep track of your expenses. (We use a program called Quicken for this purpose.) As you enter each payment, the program asks for an expense category (no fair getting cash for everything). You can then run reports to see how much was spent in each category. This is very enlightening.

Quicken is not the only program that offers these features. Among others, there are Microsoft Money; You Need A Budget Pro—Personal Finance Software Program; and Crown Financial's Crown Money Map Financial Software. None of these programs provides a ready-made budget, nor is buying a program necessary to construct a budget or track expenses. You can do it manually with paper and pencil. But whether you use paper or a software program, keeping track of expenses will save you a lot of time and effort in maintaining your family budget.

The second step is to list your usual sources and amount of income for each month. If you have a fluctuating income, such as commissions, take an average over the past six months, or budget using the base amount/lowest amount as the source for bare essentials (rent, food, utilities), and use the extra commissions for everything else. If the extra commissions exceed your needs that month, put the extra aside for the lean months.

Once you have an idea of your expenses and income, then you can plan. The first thing you must do is see if the income matches the expenses. If the expenses are greater, then some limits need to be put on your spending. Of course, there are some expenses you cannot reduce because they are fixed. This book focuses on the adjustable expenses, with groceries being the most variable. I found money for the fixed expenses by taking it out of the adjustable expenses. Other changes may need to be made, such as selling a car with a high monthly payment and buying a less expensive or used car instead.

To know if you are even close to a healthy budget, consult the experts. Larry Burkett made recommendations for household budgets in his 1993 pamphlet *A Guide to Family Budgeting.* I know this was written a while ago, but what I love about this information is that it was written in percentages and not dollar amounts. So instead of saying you should spend only eighty dollars per week on food, he says you should spend 12 percent of your income on food. This makes it more flexible than most suggested budgets.

His suggestions may not match the cost of living for your area, but this is a place to begin. I personally find the amount for housing too low, as many families spend as much as 50 percent of their budget on housing. If this is your case, giving something up in another category may be necessary. Here are his suggestions:

Larry Burkett's Suggested Budget
(after taxes and tithe)

- 38% Housing (rent/mortgage, utilities, phone, household needs)
- 12% Food
- 15% Cars (maintenance, payments)
- 5% Debts
- 5% Insurance (life and homeowner's)
- 5% Medical/Dental (bills and insurance)
- 5% Entertainment (includes cable TV)
- 5% Clothing
- 5% Savings
- 5% Miscellaneous

This is just a sample of the many learning tips available for budgeting. I have done a more exhaustive discussion of the topic in my book *Frugal Families—Making the Most of Your Hard-Earned Money*. Instead of repeating the information here, I recommend you consult the book for more details. The book can be found for free in your local library, or look for the inexpensive e-book version.

GET ORGANIZED

Now that you have a plan (or budget) for your money, you need to know what bills need to be paid and when. Entering it all into a computer program is great, but if you don't know where the bills are or you forget to pay them on time, you will spend precious cash on late fees.

Put all your bills in one place. Every time the mail arrives, sort it. You don't have to open each envelope to do this. Just put all the bills in one location—immediately as they arrive. By doing this, you reduce the risk of misplacing a bill and forgetting about it.

On every month of your calendar or date book, write down when you need to pay your bills. Most of my bills are due in the first ten days of the month, so on the thirtieth of every month, I write, "Pay bills." This way I don't forget to pay them, and I avoid late fees.

Have a checklist of bills that are to be paid every month. As you pay each bill, check it off on your list. Make sure all bills have arrived; sometimes a bill gets lost in the mail. This is no excuse for not paying it—you're still responsible for it and will be charged late fees if it doesn't get paid. If a bill hasn't arrived by bill-paying day, call the company and get the amount due and mailing address for the payment. Their phone number is on the previous month's statement. If you have set up your account for online viewing, all necessary informatin can also be found on the business's Web site. Your receipt or section of the bills that have been paid should be stored in a box or folder for record-keeping purposes. Don't throw them away: they come in handy for taxes, duplicate charge disputes, and other various reasons.

You also need to keep track of how you are doing with your spending throughout the month. Some people balance their checkbook several times a month. Others review their budget and spending every few weeks. I keep an index card in my checkbook that has eight columns—one for each major budget category that I might use while away from the house. At the top of each column I write the amount budgeted in that category. Every time I write a check, I record the amount in the appropriate column. Once the numbers in that column add up to what is budgeted for the month, I can't spend any more in that category. If I borrow from another column, I must be sure I can do without that amount in that category for the rest of the month.

By keeping track in this way, there are no surprises at the end of the month, like overdraft fees. We cannot "hope" that we will stay within our budget. We must actively make it happen. If these steps don't work for you, read the "Making it Work" section of this chapter.

DEBT REDUCTION

Debt is usually one of the main obstacles to balancing a budget. The car payment, the mortgage payment, and credit-card payments take a good share of the average household income. Once these are under control, life becomes less stressful. Most people have several credit cards, a department store card, and gas cards. In the U.S., the average household personal debt (not including mortgages) is anywhere from $8,000 to $22,000 (depending on the survey that you read). Americans are spending 132 percent of what they earn. One in seven cardholders say they are "in over their heads." We need to get this under control.

The first step is to learn to live within the boundaries of our income. Stop using credit cards for anything other than a true emergency; eating out and buying new clothes are not emergencies.

Don't rush out and cut up all your cards. Sometimes they are necessary (for renting a car or making hotel reservations). Instead, keep only one card, and control your spending. If you are using credit cards regularly and not paying them off in full each month, then you are outside of your budget and need to put the cards away in a safe place. If you are unable to control your credit-card use, don't carry them with you (unless you travel). Regard them as emergency tools only. You should carry only a debit card. Most situations allow you to go home to get the card if credit (not debit) is really necessary. Once you have reestablished some self-control, start carrying one credit card with you for emergencies. For more on credit-card use, read chapter 26, "Five Things I Wish I Knew About Money When I Was Younger."

Second, start rethinking the debts you have. Do you have a car payment that is more than you can afford? Maybe you need a less expensive car. Can you refinance for a lesser rate? Can you trade down on the car?

Third, make a plan to repay your debts. You must get rid of the debt as quickly as possible. If it takes a few years, don't despair. It's those small yet faithful steps that will get you to your goal of financial freedom. Several organizations offer tools and free help to assess your debts and make a plan to deal with them. One plan I like is offered by *CNNMoney .com*. Their tool will ask you for information about your debts and help you to see when you can get out of debt. You'll have a chance to compare your current situation against your new plan and make adjustments. Visit them at *http://cgi.money .cnn.com/tools/debtplanner/debtplanner.jsp*.

Fourth, get rid of any high-interest-rate cards. Keep only one multipurpose credit card and make it one with no annual fee. For a list of credit cards with the lowest fees and interest rates, visit the Web site *http://cardtrack.com/cards*.

Fifth, consolidate your bills to the lowest interest rate available. This may be the one credit card you have, or it may be a loan from your credit union or savings and loan. Some people consolidate their loans and then refinance their homes so their overall monthly payments are lower. This is okay if you already were going to refinance the home due to lower interest rates. Nevertheless, beware: Sometimes this new lower total payment is deceptive. Even though the combined payments are lower, the overall balance of debt may now be higher, since you added the high expense of refinancing (points, fees, etc.), and you have just reset the clock on your mortgage back thirty years. I know of families who are unable to retire, realizing the mortgage they kept refinancing is too high to pay on a pension. For more on mortgage do's and don'ts, see that section below.

Sixth, faithfully pay as much as you can each month—or more. If a little extra cash comes your way, use it toward the debt. Every little bit helps.

Finally, if you are in over your head, turn to a professional for help. There are credit counseling agencies everywhere. Be careful in choosing the right agency. Some agencies are actually interested in selling you their product or service instead of helping you. Shop around and compare services and fees. Here are some key things to look for:

- **Is the agency affiliated with a national organization?** Check to see if the agency is associated with a credible national organization. One of the better ones is the National Foundation for Credit Counseling (NFCC). They require strict financial and ethical standards for membership. Also check to see that the actual counselor you work with is certified.

- **Is the agency REALLY a nonprofit organization?** Calling itself a nonprofit organization does not guarantee that the agency is really nonprofit. Ask if they are a 501(c)(3) nonprofit organization.

- **What services does the agency offer?** You are looking for a wide range of services and not just one type or "niche" service. If the agency offers only one type of service (usually a debt-management plan), it isn't a true credit counseling service. Many counselors get compensated for writing such a plan, so they'll offer only that option. Look for budget counseling, debt counseling, housing counseling for all types of financial situations, and bankruptcy counseling, which is currently required by law. Do they offer classes to help educate consumers? The lack of classes would be a red flag.

- **What are the fees?** Watch out for any agency that charges you a fee up front. Fees are often disguised as "contributions" to the nonprofit agency. The up-front fees are often requested to pay for your credit report. Don't accept that explanation: Credit reports are free once a year to every individual. The agency should be up-front about all of their fees. Acceptable monthly charges should be twenty-five to fifty dollars or less, and the agency should be willing to waive fees in cases of hardship.

- **Will the agency work with any creditor?** Some agencies work only with creditors who make a payment to them. A legitimate agency will work with any company.

- **Minimum debt?** True credit counseling agencies will work with anyone, regardless of the size of your debt.

- **Take the time.** Ask how long the initial session will last. If it's less than an hour, keep shopping. A short interview might actually be a scoping session to see if they can sell you a product.

- **Are they listening?** If the counselor is talking more than listening, he or she might be there to sell you something rather than to help.

- **Check it out.** Check with the Better Business Bureau to see if there have been any complaints about the company.

- **Where's the money?** The full amount should go toward

the repayment of your debts, with no portion going into the agency's pocket.

- **Are you protected?** Ask for written evidence that the agency is bonded or insured. This protects you from fraud as well as shields you from any financial difficulties (like a lawsuit) that the agency might come under.

For a referral to a nonprofit credit counselor near you, contact the National Foundation for Consumer Credit at (800) 388-2227, *www.nfcc.org*, or Christian Credit Counselors, Inc., at (800) 557-1985, *www.ibudget.org*.

Mortgage Do's and Don'ts

With today's economy, people are having trouble making payments. Some are refinancing while others are giving up. Here are some do's and don'ts for your mortgage.

- If you are low on money and can't pay all the bills, don't skip the mortgage payment. Your home is an investment with equity built up every month. If the bank forecloses, they keep all of that equity.

- Don't go into foreclosure even if you have more debt than equity. This stays on your record for years and does tremendous damage to your ability to even rent again.

- Don't refinance too soon: The rule of thumb for when you should refinance is when the rates drop at least 1 percentage point below your current rate.

- Don't refinance too often. Each time you refinance you are adding up to $5,000 (in fees) to your new loan amount.

- Don't rely on the Internet or ads for your refinance company. Research the refinance company well. In many states, anyone (even those with criminal backgrounds) can open a refinance company. They could mishandle your personal information or incorrectly process your legal paper work. One company disposed of old records in the local Dumpster. Contact the Better Business Bureau, your state (or local) banking commissioner, or even the AARP for consumer complaints. A good mortgage company should mainly process new home purchases and do only about 20 percent refinances.

- Don't automatically accept the title company that your lender suggests. Research their fees and background with others.

- Work with your current lender before refinancing: It may save you thousands. To keep your business they may rework your loan.

- Avoid "quitclaim deeds" if at all possible. These are a quick transfer of the rights to the property over to you. They seem wonderful on the surface since they don't require a lot of paper work, fees, or waiting, but they only transfer whatever rights the signer has to the home (so they may not be complete rights to the home and land). They also do not allow for inspections of the home, and they offer zero recourse if you were sold a problem home. They are convenient for certain types of transfers of property, such as between family members.

- Avoid adjustable mortgage rates or balloon payments. These sneak up on you later and cause many people to lose their homes due to inability to handle the change when it comes.

- Shop around for refinance costs. Many fees vary by a thousand dollars. If they charge you no "points" but a higher interest rate, do the math yourself to see if it's a good deal or not. One point is equal to 1 percent of your loan amount.

- Insist on a rate lock or "float down," which means that your quoted rate won't go up, but it can drop if the lending rates drop.

- Make sure your current lender will not charge you a penalty for paying the loan off early. They have the legal right to, so check first.

MAKING IT WORK

For those who cannot control their spending, I suggest you leave your checkbook and credit cards at home. Put the budgeted cash into envelopes if you have to. Take the money out of the bank on a weekly basis and keep it in separate envelopes for each category in the budget. When the envelope is empty, you will have to wait until the next week.

Some financial experts have marketed items to help you with a cash system, but you can do it cheaper. Use small envelopes and label the top right-hand corners so it's easy to see the categories when flipping through the envelopes. Or purchase an inexpensive plastic coupon file that will fit in your purse, and label the sections. For those who want a software version of the cash envelopes, check out Crown Financial Mvelopes Personal Budgeting software (*http://crown.mvelopes.com*).

When we lost half our income, it was a matter of survival for the first year. I had to stick to a tight budget to keep from going into debt. I did whatever was necessary to remain frugal. If I had weak knees when I was near a department store or at the sight of a "sale" sign, I would turn my head. If impulse shopping at the grocery store overcame me, I shopped only once a month to avoid those temptations. The malls were too tempting for me, so I avoided them altogether. When I shared these ideas with people, some looked shocked or said, "Oh, that's just too drastic." Nothing is too drastic if your goals are important enough to you.

Resources

Appendix B lists additional books on budgeting and getting out of debt.

Debt-Free Living: How to Get Out of Debt and Stay Out, Larry Burkett (Moody Press, 2001).

How to Get Out of Debt, Stay Out of Debt, and Live Prosperously, Jerrold Mundis (Bantam Books, 2003).

Life After Debt: How to Repair Your Credit and Get Out of Debt Once and for All, Bob Hammond (Career Press, 2000).

Master Your Money, Ron Blue (Moody Press, 2004).

Saving on a Shoestring: How to Cut Expenses, Reduce Debt, Stash More Cash, Barbara O'Neill (MJF Books, 2003).

Two Incomes and Still Broke? It's Not How Much You Make, But How Much You Keep, Linda Kelley (Times Books, 1998).

GUIDELINE 3:

Keep Track of Food Prices

When I started my adventure of squeezing even more value from each dollar I spent, I thought I knew what most things cost. Someone suggested that I write prices down to see if I knew as much as I thought I did. This was the most educational activity I could ever do. Prices are not about the same everywhere.

I started to keep track of prices on foods in my local stores. At first I started writing down the regular retail price at each store for things I commonly used. Then I listed the best sale price for those items at the same store. By recording the best sale price, I created a goal for myself. For every item, I always included the size and unit price (cost per ounce or per pound) so I had an easy comparison. This is very important, as package sizes vary.

I keep this list in a small notebook that fits easily in my purse. I created columns for food types and then rows for the brand name, price, and unit of measure information. With that format, I could take a quick glance at who had the best prices. Below is a sample of what's in my notebook.

COLD BOXED CEREAL					
Store	**Brand Name**	**Retail Price**	**Unit Price**	**Best Sale**	**Best Unit Cost**
Store A	Store-brand "Cheerios"	16 oz. @ $2.24	14¢/oz.	12 oz. @ $1.00	8¢/oz.
Store B	Cheerios	14 oz. @ $4.42	32¢/oz.	14 oz. @ $1.99	14¢/oz.
Warehouse Club	Cheerios	37 oz. @ $4.95	14¢/oz.	no sales	14¢/oz.

By breaking items down to their unit price, I can see at a glance where an item is the least expensive. And surprisingly (to many people), it isn't cheapest at the warehouse store (more on that in chapter 16, "Be Wary of Warehouse Clubs").

From this list I began creating goals for myself. I try not to buy an item for more than the best sale price that I have seen. This becomes my target. If we don't have a target to aim for, we settle for what's available. For those of you just starting out, I have included a sample of some of my target prices. This is meant to help you get started in your shopping. These prices are an average of prices in most areas. Your region may have higher or lower prices throughout the year. On several of the items, I had to change the description from "per box" to "per ounce," since the package sizes have changed significantly. For more on this marketing trick read chapter 18, "Marketing Tricks That You Need to Know."

PRICE GOALS			
Food Item	Once in a Blue Moon	A Good Sale	Average Price
Ground beef (per lb.)	$1.99	$2.49	$3.29
Ground turkey (per lb.)	.99	1.19	3.29
Chicken (parts, per lb.)	.99	1.29	1.49
Chicken breast—boneless, skinless (per lb.)	1.79	1.88	5.49
Pork chops (per lb.)	1.00	2.99	3.69
Tuna (per oz., canned)	.10	.15	.20
Tuna (per oz., pouch)	.14	.24	.28
Milk (1 gal.)	2.50	3.50	3.85
Dry cereal (per oz.)	.08	.11	.16
Granola (per oz.)	.12	.15	.18
Butter (per lb.)	1.88	2.50	3.50
Toilet paper (per roll)	.20	.35	.83
Paper towels (per roll)	.75	1.07	2.60
Apples (per lb.)	1.00	1.69	1.99
Potatoes (per lb.)	.25	.50	1.00
Vegetable oil (per oz.)	.15	.25	.34
Olive oil (per oz.)	.25	.28	.33
Cheese (per lb.)	1.99	3.50	3.99
Flour (5 lb.)	2.00	2.50	3.19
Sugar (5 lb.)	1.99	2.29	3.29
Eggs (1 dozen)	.99	1.63	3.26
Spaghetti (1 lb.)	1.00	1.29	1.79
Cake mix	1.00	1.29	2.69
Macaroni and cheese (generic)	.50	.75	1.29

PRICE GOALS			
Food Item	**Once in a Blue Moon**	**A Good Sale**	**Average Price**
Peanut butter (per oz.)	$0.12	$0.14	$0.18
Frozen juice concentrate	1.25	1.99	2.50
Salad dressing (per oz.)	.10	.12	.28
Turkey lunch meat (per oz.)	.19	.24	.39
Lettuce (head)	1.50	2.00	2.99
Broccoli (head)	.79	.99	1.99
Light bulbs (ea.)	.25	.50	.75
Laundry detergent (per oz.)	.06	.08	.12
Facial tissue (per sheet)	.0075	.01	.0175

I set target prices in other areas as well. I know at what price I can get something, and I avoid paying much more for it. For example, I know that a homemade dinner for four people usually costs me four to five dollars. This is easy to achieve. Having this goal keeps me from ordering a twenty-dollar pizza or spending thirty-five dollars for dinner at a restaurant. You can do the same with other categories, such as clothing or toys. I have included some of my cost goals for meals to help you begin setting goals for yourself.

COST GOALS

Snacks

Key to saving in this area: Buy only one family-sized snack item per week—when it's gone, they have to wait!

- Make homemade instead of store-bought (popcorn, popcorn balls, pumpkin bread, cinnamon toast, cookies)

- Eat fruit and veggies with dips (homemade)
- Visit day-old bread outlets for cookies, chips, and crackers

Price Goal: 10¢ to 20¢ per person/per snack

Breakfast

Key to saving in this area: Avoid (or reduce use of) boxed cereals and prepackaged mixes.

- Make homemade alternatives (muffins, pancakes from scratch, French toast, eggs, hot cereal). Make them one to two times per month and freeze for easy morning use.

Price Goal: 50¢ per person/per meal

Lunch

Key to saving in this area: Avoid mixes and pre-made foods.

- Avoid fast food and other restaurants
- Make homemade sandwiches with lunch meat on sale
- Make homemade soups
- Avoid juice boxes—put homemade juice in a reusable container
- Instead of chips and cookies purchased in small bags, buy them in bulk and put some in a small plastic bag.
- Use leftovers from other meals

Price Goal: $1.25 per person/per meal

Notes: Invest in a lunchbox-size freezer pack so the kids can take perishable items to school (tuna sandwich, lunch meat, leftovers). Also invest in a small reusable container for soup and one for juice.

INTERESTING FACTOIDS

Price differences since seven years ago

Little to Moderate Change

Chicken breasts (when on sale)
Toilet paper (when on sale)
Sugar (when on sale)

Moderate to Large Change

Flour (doubled)
Fruit (doubled)
Butter (doubled)
Vegetables (tripled)
Pasta (tripled)
Most paper products (tripled)

Dinner

Key to saving in this area: Avoid convenient mixes and pre-made foods.

- Avoid fast food and other restaurants
- Stretch the meat with vegetables, whole grains, and beans

Price Goals: Budget meal for four: $2 total
Average meal for four: $4 total
Special meal (seafood, roast) for four: $10+ total

GUIDELINE 4:

Don't Buy Everything at the Same Store

Of the eleven guidelines, I believe this one has been the greatest source of savings for me. Although planning for and shopping at several stores is the biggest time expenditure in the "job" of being miserly, it provides the biggest payoff. It can save you up to 50 percent of your grocery bill and take very little time.

No one store has the lowest price on everything—not even the warehouse clubs. As I learn more about the art of being miserly, my bills keep dropping. There are two main stages to shopping: planning and deciding where to buy. If you do these two stages while rolling through the grocery aisles, you won't save anything. You must become aware of who sells what, and what each item costs. You can incorporate coupons and rebates, but they must be secondary to where and what you decide to buy. Below is an explanation of how I do my planning and shopping.

PLANNING

The worst mistake shoppers make is to show up at the grocery store and simply buy whatever they think they'll need that week. Planning is essential to your savings success. Even if you choose to do all of your shopping in one store, just having a list will reduce your spending. Most people think of planning as picking their menus for the week, making a list, and buying those things at the nearest store. I want to challenge you to rethink your planning and shopping process.

Instead of making a random menu plan and shopping around it, plan the menu and lists around the grocery sales. One friend of mine saved thirty dollars the first time she switched her planning style. She didn't apply any of the other tips in the book. She just planned the menu around the sale items instead of picking recipes randomly.

The best way to prepare for a shopping trip is to read the sale flyers from local grocery stores. These are often found in the food section of the newspaper. You can also see them online by visiting the store's Web site (e.g., *www.safeway.com* or *www.vons.com*). Some Web sites have compiled these sales for you. One such site that offers this service for free is *www.mygrocerydeals.com*. Start by entering your zip code and the stores that you want it to review, and a customized list of deals is made for you.

Once you find the deals, build a menu plan around these sale items. The items on the front and back pages are called *loss leaders*, because the store is losing money on those items. By making those items the base of your menu, you can save up to 35 percent on groceries. Instead of arbitrarily deciding to have pork chops, meatloaf, and fried chicken this week, I let the sale items determine what we'll have. Don't forget to plan your produce needs around those loss leaders as well. The key to making this work is to offer your family variety. I do this by using several cookbooks that have a good index for looking up the type of meat I'm using. I save even more if my menus are based on low-cost recipes found in frugal cookbooks.

Don't think this means that dinner is going to get repetitive. Even if—and this rarely happens—only one type of meat is on sale that week in all stores, you can still make seven frugal and different meals. For example, if chuck roast is all that is available, you can make pot roast, beef stew, fajitas, chili, tacos, pulled beef sandwiches, and beef stroganoff . . . and your family will never know they had the same meat all week. (Chicken can be substituted for each of these seven meals.) Another idea is to cook all the meat the first night, then bag it into meal-sized portions and freeze it for the rest of the week's meals.

After I make my menus based on sale items, I make grocery lists for each store. And if there is no great loss leader available, I use what I have stored from a previous bulk buy and skip that week's loss leaders.

COUPONS AND REBATES

Coupons can be helpful for saving money when we use them wisely and don't let them direct us.

Some people are opposed to using coupons under any circumstances. Their reasons vary, but the most common complaint is that coupons increase the price of food because the manufacturer must recover the costs somewhere. This is a valid concern, but boycotting coupons will not drive the prices back down again.

Many manufacturers won't drop coupons for that reason. Even though only 3 percent of consumers use coupons, manufacturers continue to spend millions of dollars printing and distributing them. Coupons cost them less than reducing their prices. They believe that a coupon is a discount available for those who want to make the extra effort, and for maintaining good relations with those same (but few) consumers.

I have noticed that coupons are usually for name-brand

convenience foods. Rarely do you see a coupon for meat, bread, or milk. With a coupon, I am tempted to buy something that I normally would not buy—just because I have a coupon. When I am tempted to buy an item because I have a coupon, I ask myself three questions: (1) Do I need it? (2) Can I buy it cheaper in another brand? (3) Can I prepare it cheaper myself?

It's important to compare the price of the name-brand item (less the coupon) to the price of an off-brand item without a coupon. Even with a coupon, the name-brand item may still cost more than the off-brand item. And the off-brand items are not inferior in most cases. Actually, many off-brand items are name-brand items that have been repackaged and relabeled for that store.

Coupons can be very helpful. A good sale matched with a coupon can be a good deal. And it can be an even greater deal if a store offers double coupons and has a sale at the same time. Or the store may be having a buy one, get one free sale and they offer double coupons. But be aware that most stores offering double or triple coupons have higher prices on most of their groceries. I usually purchase the items I have good coupons for and take the rest of my list somewhere else.

Take advantage of the coupon books mailed out by stores. These stores hope to draw you in with your entire week's grocery list. If you buy just the coupon items, you can save big. Remember to take the rest of your list to the cheapest store nearby. With these coupon books, I make a monthly trip to stock up on cereals, soups, and other items. Each time I make this trip with the coupon book, I get thirty to forty dollars taken off at the register.

You can maximize your savings if you use a manufacturer's coupon (issued by the food manufacturer) at the same time you use a store coupon. For example, the store selling Cheerios for $3.99 may also be having a buy one, get one free sale. You have a $1.00-off-two-boxes cash register (store) coupon from your last visit and a manufacturer's coupon from the Sunday newspaper for $1.50 off two boxes. Using all three deals is a real steal (two boxes for $1.49, or 75¢ each)!

Places to find good coupons are the Sunday newspapers, local library coupon exchange boxes, local coupon clubs, and even the Internet. If your library doesn't have an exchange box, ask if you can start one. Visit Web sites that allow you to print your own grocery coupons, such as Smart Source (*www .smartsource.com*) and Cool Savings (*www.coolsavings.com*). Many coupon sites offer printable coupons. Avoid any Web sites that charge a fee for usage or offer bank account credit instead of free coupons.

Another good way to get coupons of high value is to write a note of appreciation (or complaint) to the manufacturer of a product you use. They usually send several valuable coupons for your trouble.

Once you have some coupons, keep them in a small portable filing system. I use a small expandable folder. I file by food category (snacks, breakfast, side dishes, vegetables, desserts, household items, baby items). Some people file alphabetically or by expiration date. Do whatever works best for you. However, the method won't do you any good unless you make sure the coupons are with you when you shop. One friend of mine gathers the coupons she'll need for that shopping trip and staples them to the shopping list so they won't be forgotten at home. I have given my list and coupons to my husband and seen him forget them at checkout time, so I have been known to staple the coupons to the check in the checkbook so there is no way he can forget.

Rebates can also be good, especially if matched with a sale and coupons. You may have heard stories of people spending only $20 for $120 worth of groceries by combining coupons, sales, and rebates. It can be done, but this is a rare event. And it isn't much of a savings if you have to buy things you normally wouldn't buy just to get a rebate. There are avid rebate fans who spend up to twenty hours per week reading rebate newsletters and clipping, mailing, and filing grocery receipts and proof-of-purchase seals. I can't help but repeat myself—would I buy these things anyway? It would be cheaper (and take less time) to shop sales and cook more meals from scratch.

Overall, I do not encourage an excessive emphasis on coupons or rebates. There are coupon clubs and subscriber services for coupons/rebates. I think you eventually lose with these. The real savings is following the lowest price—whether that is a sale or an off-brand. Occasionally that lowest price may be the use of a coupon plus a sale. Then it is to your advantage. Remember that coupons and rebates are one of the many tools to help you get to your savings goal.

To illustrate this point, let me tell you about a shopping competition I participated in. I was invited to be a guest on the TV talk show *The Gayle King Show*. I was there to compare my shopping style with another "grocery expert." The other expert was the creator of the Coup-O-Dex coupon filing system (a Rolodex made for coupons that rests on the grocery cart's handle). He believed in using coupons for everything he could. We were both assigned a family to plan and shop for, and we both did our shopping and met at the checkout counter (with cameras following our every move). When he checked out, he had $46 worth of coupons taken off his bill, leaving him with a final food bill of $72. When I checked out, I had no coupons, but my food bill was only $49. How? I had planned meals around the sale items, bought off-brands, and avoided convenience foods. He planned the meals around the coupons he had, which tend to be for the more expensive name-brand and convenience items.

SHOPPING

Once my planning is done, I go to each store and buy only those items on my list. I first visit the more expensive stores and buy their good sale items on my list. Don't impulse buy. Don't look up and down the aisles for what's available. Again, it's important to remember that those stores with the greatest sale prices (or loss leaders) and double or triple coupons tend to have higher prices on everything else. Their sale prices are great, but their other items tend to be 20 percent higher than most stores. They have to recover their losses somewhere. This is why it is important to buy only their sale items. I go to two or three stores this way, getting the sale items I need for my menus. My last store is the one I find to be cheapest overall and buy their sale items and the rest of my grocery list.

Many people might say, "Why spend all that time going from store to store? A few cents saved at one store won't pay for the gas of hopping around." It's not just "a few cents" being saved, as you'll quickly realize after one week's worth of shopping. You might lose your savings if you drove long distances to the two or three stores that you choose, but all the stores should be within ten miles of your home, so gas isn't an issue. I figure—even with today's high gasoline prices—that I save thirty to fifty dollars in groceries with each shopping trip and only use four to six dollars in gas.

I usually do all the shopping in one afternoon, as it is easier to finish all at once. Take a few days if it works better for you. Shop one store on the way home from somewhere. The short lists only take fifteen to twenty minutes. Or send your hubby to one of the stores with a precise list. Some weeks I find only two or three items on sale that interest me at the "secondary" stores. When this happens, I skip those stores that week. It has to pay off to go to the extra stores if you are going to do it.

Beware of the "great" sale! Sometimes a store announces a big-name item at a great price, but they only offer one of its products at that price. For example, a store once advertised Oscar Mayer hot dogs at $1.50. The average store price was $2.49. But only one of Oscar Mayer's three types of hot dogs was offered at this price. The other two were overpriced at $3.99 each. Watch the fine print. There are certain stores that do this type of advertising regularly. If the store that you frequent is always out of the sale item, drop it from your shopping routine. Many stores purchase a limited stock of the sale item, hoping you will purchase a more expensive substitute. Ask for a rain check. Some stores won't give one until the last day of the sale. So shop there on the last day to get what's in stock and get the rest next week with the rain check.

TYPES OF STORES

You aren't alone in working to reach your goal. There are many types of stores to help the miserly mom. There are warehouse clubs, supermarkets, grocery outlets, specialty outlet stores, and more. They can make your job easier and hopefully help you stay on track. You must know how and when to use them. Let's look at each type of store.

Warehouse Clubs

The warehouse club stores, such as Costco or Sam's Club, can save you money—but only on certain things. I see people buying everything they need at these stores, thinking all their items are cheaper. You must know your prices before you shop there. Because this type of store is so popular, yet tricky to use, I have set aside an entire chapter to discuss its use (chapter 16, "Be Wary of Warehouse Clubs"). The bottom line: Shop sparingly at these stores.

Supermarket Warehouses

There are supermarket warehouses that offer bulk foods and minimal services (such as no baggers) to cut costs. Some of these might be Pak'n Save, Cub Foods, Grocery Warehouse, Rainbow Foods, and Food-4-Less. Some of these stores carry a limited variety of name brands compared to regular grocery stores, but they do have good prices. This is where I usually take the rest of my list. The only items that I have had quality trouble with are meats, fish, milk, and open bins of bulk foods (people put odd things in them). If you have small children, shopping at these can be stressful because you have to bag your own food, pay for it, and care for the kids all at the same time.

Outlet Stores

There are also outlet stores that sell clothing, food, or specialty items at discount prices. These stores are usually listed by their company name (e.g., Oshkosh, Nike, Wonder, Hostess, Entenmann's, Oroweat, etc.). These are great places to find good bargains. The clothing outlets usually are not cheaper than a department store sale, but their clearance racks are great. The bread stores oftentimes have half-price loaves of bread and other baked goods. Many have a "cheap" day when items are 10 percent off or more, and they offer frequent-buyer's cards that allow you to earn free products.

Then there are general outlet stores that carry a variety of goods. Some of these examples may be in your area:

- *Trader Joe's*, which sells food items of their own brand as well as imported items.
  Good Buys: fish, breads, cereals, vitamins, dairy

- *Canned Food Grocery Outlet*, which sells surplus, out-dated, discontinued, or dented items at good prices.
  Good Buys: all items

- *Aldi's*, which sells a variety of discounted food and goods.
  Good Buys: milk and diapers

- *Wal-Mart*, which sells a variety of goods and foods.
  Good Buys: most items
  Note: Many Wal-Mart stores will match grocery store flyer prices. The only drawback is that they don't carry many brands, so you have to negotiate a replacement brand with the clerk, who may ask you to wait for the manager. If you don't mind this hassle, it's worth it.

- *Dollar Stores*, which have good deals on food and household items.
  Good Buys: cleaning supplies, snacks, canned foods, wrapping paper, paper products, baskets, dishes, sunglasses, seasonal decorations.
  Avoid: Vitamins and medications (diluted doses), toys for infants and toddlers, cosmetics.

- *PX/Military* have good overall prices. They are usually as cheap as you can get on sale at a regular grocery store. Use these if you have access to them.

Co-ops

Another source for low-cost food is a co-op. They can provide organic (and other) products at a lower cost than most local stores. Items that you might buy in a health food store are usually—but not always—much cheaper through a co-op. This is where knowing your prices is essential.

There are many different types of co-ops, but some co-ops are formed when some friends get together to buy foods wholesale to save money. They find a wholesale co-op distributor that will allow new members in their area (many areas are closed due to retail store pressure of the competition: retail stores don't like wholesale outlets that sell the same manufacturers' goods as they do). Someone does the ordering, receives the shipment, divides the orders, and handles the money. Many groups also hold meetings and seminars on nutritional cooking.

Many co-ops have gone to a mail-order style, where you get a quarterly catalog and send in your request. These types of businesses usually sell in large quantities, such as a case of cereal boxes or potato chips. This sort of buying is good for people who consume a great deal of certain items, or who can split a case with someone. Beware of the traps of being in a co-op. Some groups require a minimum-dollar-amount purchase every month. This can be binding if you don't need to buy or don't have the grocery money for it that month. I have also found that I tend to overbuy when I'm in a co-op. Even though something may be a great price, I don't need twelve of them. I also tend to buy things at a co-op that I normally wouldn't buy—just because it is wholesome and/or a great deal. But do I really need it?

Ask friends at church or work for information about co-operatives—word of mouth is a great source. Doing a search on the Internet will also provide some local organizations that might not be listed with national ones. If none of these provide help, visit one of these sites to help you find a co-op:

- National Cooperative Business Association, *www .cooperative.org*, will give you the regional headquarters of cooperatives near you.
- Local Harvest maintains an active nationwide directory of small farms, farmers' markets, and other local food sources. Their search engine helps people find products from family farms and locally grown food, and it encourages them to establish direct contact with small farms in their local area. *www.localharvest.org/organic-farms*.

- Some kind folks at Columbia University have been compiling a list of worldwide co-ops. It is only as complete as people write in with their co-op information. *http://niany .com/food.coop.html.*

EXCHANGING SERVICES

Many people are relearning the skill of exchanging services. I say "relearning," since this was the original form of business transaction in America. The early settlers bought and sold goods by offering something they had made in exchange—such as homemade cheese for a handmade woolen item. This form of business is still around. Many do it casually by finding something they can offer and asking someone if they would consider exchanging services with them. A friend of mine wanted to join a local pool for the summer but couldn't afford it, so she offered to paint their changing rooms in exchange for her family's membership. Other friends exchange lawn care, hair care, wedding services (cakes, flowers, music, photography), auto repair, ironing, sewing, etc.

For those with more elaborate needs or who live where there are limited resources, there are national exchange or bartering groups. The groups list what you are interested in obtaining and offering. They usually charge a high annual fee for this service. I have found that many local churches offer such listings free of charge.

There are several bartering networks and clubs you can join. Some are online groups that you can barter with anywhere in the U.S. These clubs work by charging a small transaction fee for posting services or goods for trade on the network. The service keeps track of the credits you have exchanged with another member. No money is exchanged, but the value of the goods or services is recorded. For example, if you were a writer and you wrote an article for a company's magazine, and you valued your work at $600, you would have a $600 credit that you could use with any other member in the network. For a local bartering group, look in your Yellow Pages or on Craigslist.com under "Barter."

Before joining a barter network, do some research. Your reputation, as well as trade credits, is at stake. Ask how large the network is, what categories for trade are available, how long the network has been operating (look for one that's been around at least five years), and what the members think about it (write to them and ask them). There is an agency that can run a background check on network exchanges for you: the International Reciprocal Trade Association. Visit them online at *www.irta.com*. There is also the National Association of Trade Exchanges, a nonprofit organization that serves barter clubs and their members and can locate exchange networks near you (*www.nate.org*).

--------------------------  --------------------------

Personal and Business Bartering, James Harvey Stout (TAB Books, 1985).

Storefront Revolution: Food Co-Ops and the Counterculture, Craig Cox (University Press, 1994).

CHAPTER 7

GUIDELINE 5:

Buy in Bulk Whenever Possible

Buying in bulk seems logical, but there are some basic tips to know in order to make it work. There are two ways to buy in bulk: large quantities of regular-sized items or large-sized containers. The best savings are earned with a combination of both.

Two examples of buying large quantities are when I buy a whole case of paper towels when they go on sale or several loaves of bread during my monthly visit to the day-old bread store. I calculate what I will use during one month and buy that amount. I say one month because that is approximately when an item is likely to go on sale somewhere else. If you can stock up for two months at a time, you will save even more.

Buying in large containers saves money because you are reducing the packaging and handling required by the manufacturer. It is really worth it to buy in bulk and deal with the minor inconvenience of repackaging the food into meal-sized bags or finding some storage space. Getting started may be difficult because of the cost involved. Eat very cheaply the first week, and use that savings to make your first bulk purchase. Each week it will be easier.

A good example of this type of savings is buying boneless, skinless chicken breasts in bulk. Compare the prices of these different packaging types:

Chicken Breasts (Boneless/Skinless)

$5.49 per lb. Individual packages
$2.67 per lb. Warehouse club bulk
$1.99 per lb. Good sale
$1.79 per lb. Great (rare) sale

Ask friends and neighbors if they know someone who works at a meat distribution company or where you could buy meat wholesale. If this is unavailable, ask your butcher or meat department how much ground beef or turkey you would have to buy in order to get a discount. It might be forty pounds or more. Don't laugh—the price might be worth it.

Some people are concerned about the fat content of the cheaper hamburger. To tackle the fat, cook the beef, then rinse it with hot water. This gets the same result as buying expensive lean ground beef . . . and will cost you less.

If you buy the ground beef in bulk, believe it or not, you can handle all of that meat at one time. Form some of the meat into meatballs and freeze them in plastic bags (each bag is a meal portion); make a huge kettle of chili and freeze it in meal-sized portions; and pack the rest of the hamburger in one- or two-pound portions and freeze individually for later use. You can ask friends if they want to join with you in a purchase. My friend had to buy eighty pounds of ground beef to obtain a good price. We split it among four families. I didn't have an extra freezer, and I could still store it with ease. Another benefit of bulk buying is that it helps avoid running out of something and having to rush to the store to pay full price.

If you think you can't buy in bulk because you don't have the space, listen to me: When I lived in a small townhouse with no storage space, I figured out how to use the little space that I had. I used old bookshelves in the garage for a pantry. I didn't want a second freezer because of the extra cost (both the initial cost as well as the extra utility expense), so I went to the hardware store and bought a plastic-coated wire rack and put it in my tiny freezer above the refrigerator. The added shelf doubled the amount of usable freezer space. I know of people who store canned goods under beds or in hallway cupboards. I haven't had to go that far, but if you are motivated, you will be amazed at the storage space you can find.

CONTAINERS

I don't spend money on expensive storage containers. To maximize freezer space, I store my meals and food in plastic bags. When filled with a meal and flattened, the bags lie only a half-inch to an inch thick. I am able to stack several of them on top of each other. Once frozen, they can be turned sideways and stacked like books. If I used plastic containers, I would not be able to fit as many meals in my little freezer.

The cost of plastic resealable bags is minimal. I pay between one and two cents per bag by watching sales and using a coupon at the same time. I use thirty per month for main meals (that's about fifty cents per month), and I can wash many of them for reuse (but not the ones used for raw meat, eggs, or fish).

After World War II, people started demanding convenience foods. With this change, we have lost some of the wisdom of homemade foods and storage that our grandparents learned. People who went through the Great Depression let nothing go to waste. Food containers were saved. Everything was put to a new use. Even the flour sacks were used to make dresses (the material was soft cotton with a floral print). Here are some of the things we can glean from their experiences:

- Save jars (mayonnaise, syrup, etc.). Reuse them for your homemade syrups, chocolate sauces, salad dressings, etc.

- Save cardboard oatmeal boxes as storage containers for dry goods (your homemade granola, bulk items bought from bins, or small toys).

- Save cereal boxes for magazine holders (cut the side off diagonally and cover with contact paper to make more attractive).

- Use Pringles cans to ship cookies to friends. The cans reduce breakage.

- Wash out plastic mustard squeeze bottles and fill with homemade colored frosting for cake and cookie decorating.

- Reuse margarine tubs for food storage. The largest sizes available (usually five pounds) are large enough to store food for one meal. The smaller containers are good for leftovers, lunches, and side dishes.

- Reuse resealable freezer bags by washing carefully and then checking for leaks. Again, don't reuse bags that were used for raw meat, raw eggs, or fish.

GUIDELINE 6:

Make Your Own Whenever Possible

Make *your own* has been one of the most profitable of the eleven guidelines: a never-ending exploration with great rewards.

Most people believe they have to *buy* everything they need. It wasn't that long ago that we *made* everything we needed. People even made their own baking powder. Recipes for just about everything you use can be found in a cookbook somewhere. The older the book, the better. I prefer the cookbooks from the 1880s to 1950s because they had basic, simple recipes—sometimes with pictures on how to prepare things. Garage sales and libraries are great sources for these cookbooks. One of my favorite newer cookbooks is the *More-With-Less Cookbook* by Doris Longacre. This is full of recipes for simple homemade alternatives to common grocery items such as cereals, soups, breads, etc.

Depending on your source for homemade alternatives, making your own can save you more than pocket change. Some people enjoy the homey feeling that comes from cooking from scratch. If you do, then you'll benefit in more than one way from this advice. There are a few things that are cheaper to

buy than make, so I make my own only if it will save money
or if it will be more nutritious.

To get the most from my time in the kitchen, I looked at
my spending and attacked the highest expenditures first. I
reviewed four weeks' worth of grocery receipts and catego-
rized my expenditures by food type (dairy, breakfast, meat,
vegetables, snacks). I picked the most expensive type and
went to work, creatively replacing pre-made foods with homemade alternatives. Below are the types of food I began making
instead of buying. They are in order, starting with those for
which we spent the most, ending with those for which we
spent the least.

BREAKFAST

My highest expense was breakfast. We spent forty dollars
per month on this one meal—and that was in 1992. Most
families spend 25 to 30 percent of their food bill on breakfast
products, relying mostly on prepackaged cereal. We did too.
This has become a very profitable business for the manufacturers. The average box of cereal costs three to five dollars. Many
families eat two or three boxes per week. That's forty to sixty
dollars per month just for cereal. This is a worthy target for
the miserly arrow.

My first move was to introduce alternatives to cereal two
to three times per week. I don't slave in the kitchen every
morning. Once a month or so I make a double batch of muffins, banana bread, or pancakes and freeze them. It's so easy
to pop the frozen item into the toaster oven or microwave
for a meal.

Don't use prepackaged baking mixes. Since they cost four
times more to buy them, you will lose your savings on them.
Baking from scratch takes about the same amount of time as

using a baking mix. If you're addicted to these, make your own baking mix. Mixes can be stored for up to six months in the cupboard. They can be used with any Bisquick recipe you have. Here's my favorite:

Baking Mix

> 8 C. flour
> 1¼ C. nonfat dry milk powder
> ¼ C. baking powder
> 1 T. salt
> 2 C. shortening

Combine flour, milk powder, baking powder, and salt in a very large bowl. Cut in shortening until it resembles coarse cornmeal. Store in tightly closed covered container in a cool place (cupboards are fine). Makes about 10 cups.

I then experimented with recipes for cereal. I found one for Grape-Nuts, several for granola, and some for muesli-style cereal. (See chapter 15, "Some Great Recipes," for my husband's favorite granola recipe.) All were delicious and cost only a fraction of the price of store-bought versions (remember that the manufacturers have to pay for that colorful box and all that glitzy advertising). I occasionally buy boxed cereal when it is on a good sale, combined with a coupon. This way I pay only one to two dollars for a box. With these changes, I reduced my breakfast spending to twenty dollars per month. That's half! To show what a difference cooking from scratch can make, here are some cost comparisons:

Sample of Cost Comparisons		
Breakfast food	Name brand	Home-made
Granola (1 lb.)	$3.87	$1.50
Pancake syrup (24 oz.)	3.89	0.25
Frozen microwave pancakes/waffles (12)	1.99	0.45

SNACK FOODS AND DRINKS

My next highest expense was snack foods, which includes cookies, chips, fruit leather, candy, Popsicles, ice cream, and beverages. My first move was to try to introduce a homemade treat whenever a snack was needed. Candy and chips can be replaced with homemade cookies, homemade granola bars, or popcorn. Popcorn costs two cents per cup to make (the old-fashioned way), and is a healthy snack.

Popsicles bought at the store cost more than homemade ones and usually have additives you may prefer to avoid. Making them at home also is a great way to use yogurt and fruit that might spoil if left unused. Here are some ideas:

• Puree fruits that are getting a bit mushy or overripe in a blender. This works well with watermelon, strawberries, and bananas. To jazz it up, add some chocolate chips to the molds.

• Mix plain yogurt with the ripe fruits, or use fruit juice or fruit extract and a bit of sugar to taste. Pour into Popsicle molds. This is only a good buy if the yogurt is on sale or needs to be used soon.

• Flat soda pop makes great Popsicles. My favorite is root beer.

- If you made or bought some chai tea (ready made), this makes great Popsicles.

COFFEE

I have been a connoisseur of the brown liquid for a long time. I went so far as to have the beans imported from Hawaii because I felt these were the best-tasting beans in the world.

Here are some ideas to cut down on the cost of drinking coffee:

- Your coffeemaker at home does not get the water as hot as the commercial machines do. The extra heat gives the coffee more flavor. If you desire to get your cup of coffee as close to coffee-shop quality as possible, try boiling water in a kettle and manually pouring the water over the grounds.

- To get the most flavors from your beans, wait to grind them until you are ready to brew. And the finer the grind of coffee, the stronger the brew.

- A home-brewed cup of coffee can cost twenty-five times less than at a trendy coffee shop!

- Freeze leftover coffee in ice-cube trays and use in iced coffee drinks.

Another snack we frequently make is cookies. We enjoy making them together (and eating them together). Most people buy cookies. I have heard many people in stores say that you can't make your own any cheaper than the packaged cookies, especially when they are on sale. I often wondered if this was really true. So I took out my calculator (again) and figured the cost for chocolate chip cookies. I determined that homemade cookies usually cost half that of pre-made versions.

The most expensive ingredient is the chocolate chips, which I buy when on sale. Other types of cookies, such as oatmeal or snickerdoodles, are less expensive. To save time, I make a double or triple batch of cookie dough. I divide the dough into balls the size of a baseball and freeze each ball. Or leave in the refrigerator for up to one week. When it's baking time, I thaw one ball and bake the cookies. This way my cookies are always fresh when wanted.

We were surprised to find that 30 percent of our grocery bill was being spent on beverages . . . and this is very common. With the milk, coffee, orange juice, apple juice, and sodas we drink, it was easy to reach a high percentage of our budget. Once we saw this, we suggested that the kids drink water when they are thirsty, since that is what their bodies need anyway. We replaced soda with generic versions of Kool-Aid or other drink mixes. When frozen concentrated juices go on sale, we buy several. But our family still needs to control how much of these are consumed in a week. If we don't, we tend to drink up in a week what was supposed to last a month. One way to ration the good

---

MILK

- The cheapest way to buy milk is to buy in whole gallons. Buying a half-gallon of milk can cost you 50% more than a whole gallon. And some stores discount it more if you buy 2 gallons at a time.
- Use instant milk. The nonfat dry milk runs about $2 per gallon as opposed to $4 per gallon of fresh milk. Some families cut fresh milk with instant milk (hint: the colder the mixed milk, the better it tastes). The nutrition is the same, and the lack of fat is a plus.
- Buy whole milk and then water it down. This makes the milk taste similar to one-percent milk and can reduce the cost of a gallon of milk by half.

---

drinks is to allow only one cup of juice or milk at meals, and water after that if they are still thirsty. Or you could allow only water at mealtimes and juice after the food is finished. This way they don't fill up on the drinks and skimp on the food.

The average American household consumes sixteen quarts of soft drinks or juices per month (two bottles of two-liter sodas per week). If we calculate the cost over one month for each of these, it really adds up: Some people spend fifty dollars per month on beverages alone. Next to water, it is much cheaper (up to ten times cheaper!) to serve instant drink mixes than sodas.

Another beverage we make is smoothies. We put some fruit in a blender (strawberries, peaches, bananas, kiwi, oranges, or whatever we have on hand) and add some liquid (apple juice or milk) and blend until smooth. For a thicker texture, add ice or frozen fruit, replace the milk with yogurt, and blend. It's refreshing, healthy, yummy, and an inexpensive alternative to the high-priced juice shops that sell these for five to eight dollars each.

MEATS

Another high expense for many families is meat. I cut meat costs in three ways: buy it in bulk, "stretch" it, and replace it with nutritious alternatives.

A few years ago I read about a woman who had a target price for meat of one dollar per pound. I laughed when I read this and wondered how I could ever share that goal. Then I began to watch the ads. With the recent price changes, it's not very likely I'll find ground beef that inexpensive, but hamburger does occasionally go on sale for $1.99 per pound (in bulk packaging). I buy these and slice them into one-pound portions and freeze them. When you need a pound, pull one out. Ground turkey sometimes goes on sale for ninety-nine cents a pound. Scan the sale flyers each week. I have seen pork chops, ribs, and chicken quarters for as little as ninety-nine cents a pound.

For leaner meat, buy a roast on sale and have it ground. You can also go in with a few friends and buy the higher-grade meats in bulk from your butcher or meat department at a good discount.

At Thanksgiving many stores offer a lower price on turkey during the few days before that feasting Thursday. I can usually buy a turkey when they are on sale for seventy-nine cents per pound. Stock up with as many as your freezer can handle. I try to buy as large a bird as I can fit into my oven, and then I'll have leftovers for a week or more at very little cost or effort. After we eat our Thanksgiving meal, I cut the meat off of the bone and freeze meal-sized portions. I use the best cuts for turkey sandwiches or turkey fillets. As the week progresses, I serve the smaller pieces in stir-fry or Creole-type dishes. When I get down to the bone, I make soup. Nothing goes to waste. Here are some turkey buying and cooking tips to assist you:

- Plan on one pound of turkey per person. This does not allow for leftovers, however.

- A tom is the male turkey and is usually tougher (but larger). A hen is the female and is usually smaller and more tender.

- To thaw a turkey in the refrigerator, plan ahead. Thawing takes about twenty-four hours for every five pounds of turkey.

- To thaw a bird in the sink, cover with cold water and allow approximately twelve hours for large birds and approximately five hours for smaller ones. Remember to change the water often, keeping it cold.

- Many cookbooks recommend roasting turkey breast-side up. I prefer to roast my birds breast-side down. This allows the juices to run down into the breast, making the meat more tender and juicy.

- Loosely cover the top of the bird with foil. This keeps it from browning too much and drying out.

- Don't keep opening the oven to peek at the bird. You let heat escape each time and lengthen the baking time.

- For a gourmet touch, rub the skin with half of an orange. Do this close to the end of the roasting or it will burn.

Stretching your meat is a good way to reduce expenses. Adding a nutritious filler stretches the meat's volume while keeping its nutritional value. Two fillers that work well and are nutritious are boiled wheat kernels and TVP. Boiled wheat is simply whole-wheat kernels (found at health food stores and some grocery stores) that have been boiled until soft. TVP is a soy product that looks and feels like ground beef but has no flavor. It assumes the flavor of the seasonings you add. It is dried and is reconstituted by mixing equal parts of hot water and TVP. Both fillers are low in fat, inexpensive (each costs around forty cents a pound when cooked), and high in fiber. Whichever filler you choose, use an equal amount of filler to hamburger. One family I know keeps a container of boiled wheat kernels in their refrigerator ready for any meal preparation.

Another way we beat the high cost of meat is by replacing meat with vegetables, grains, legumes, or beans. This will lower your fat intake and help you with your "five-a-day" consumption. (Nutritional guidelines recommend at least five servings of fruits and vegetables per day.) By using healthy alternative all-grain recipes, you can feed a family of four for one dollar. I have even found several lentil-rice, veggie burger, and rice-and-bean recipes that my picky eaters like. I am not suggesting you become a vegetarian. Rather, I recommend that you replace a few meals per week with a non-meat or low-meat dish. Some ideas are stir-fry, egg-and-rice casseroles, and potato-based dishes. My book *Healthy Meals for Less* has a chapter filled with our family's favorite meatless recipes.

Eggs are another way to fulfill your protein needs, but for less money than meat. Eggs cost eight to ten cents each when on sale. A quiche dish for four requires four to six eggs plus a few other ingredients and costs about one dollar. Other egg-based dishes that are low-cost are frittata, soufflé, egg salad sandwiches, fried rice with egg, egg drop soup, and omelets (yes, it's okay to eat them for dinner). Eggs freeze well when taken out of the shell, so buy them in bulk when on sale.

Here is a price comparison list of meat alternatives:

- steak dinner for four = $15 to $20
- fish fillets for four = $10 to $15
- hamburger dinner for four = $7 to $9
- stir-fry dinner for four = $5 to $6
- quiche for four = $2
- rice and beans for four = $2
- lentil-rice casserole for four = $1

For more information on meat alternatives, see chapter 10, "Cut Back on Meats."

PRODUCE

The last high expense I noticed was produce. While you don't want to skimp on vegetables and fruit, there are ways to reduce their costs. Supermarkets make 30 percent of their overall profit from their produce section. Once I learned this, I knew there had to be cheaper ways to buy fresh produce.

The first way to save money is to grow your own. If you have yard space that isn't being used, make it work for you (instead of you working for it by mowing, weeding, etc.). I have a friend who converted her lawn into a huge vegetable garden. She doesn't buy much produce anymore. When you grow your own, the vegetables cost about one to five cents each. For more information on how to set up a productive garden for little money, see chapter 17, "Stretch the Season."

The next best thing I did was take advantage of the farmers' markets. The prices are often (not always) great! Much of the produce is organic as well as very fresh. Most of the items are allowed to vine-ripen, making them more nutritious. Go at the end of the day and get even better savings. Many farmers don't want to take anything back home with them and are willing to sell cheaply. If you are able to can or freeze, buy extra vegetables and fruit. You'll have plenty of produce on hand, and you'll be able to beat the high off-season prices at the supermarkets. Below is a list of what's commonly found "in season" at a farmers' market. Since things are cheaper when they are in season, plan your menus around in-season foods and reduce the cost of your meals.

Seasonal Produce Savings

- **Summer:** grapes, tomatoes, plums, avocadoes, zucchini, peaches, melons
- **Fall:** apples, winter squash, oranges, pumpkins, broccoli, melons
- **Winter:** broccoli, oranges, acorn squash
- **Spring:** berries, asparagus, bananas, plums, lettuce
- **Year round:** potatoes, carrots, celery

If any of these foods aren't available in your area of the country or you can't get to a farmers' market, the next best thing is to stock up on fresh or frozen vegetables on sale. One of my local grocery chains has an annual dollar sale on produce. This is a great way to get your five-a-day. I stock up on whatever is being sold, freezing the produce for future use. Since some produce needs preparation before freezing, consult the experts. There are some suggested books on this topic at the end of this chapter.

It's best to eat fresh produce to obtain the right nutrients, but unless you grow your own or buy organic produce, frozen vegetables can be a close second to fresh. They are flash frozen and bagged after being blanched.

The last and least desirable way to save on produce is to buy canned fruits and vegetables. We don't do this too often since canned produce has been cooked and salted, leaving fewer nutrients than fresh produce. Many nutrients are heat sensitive, getting lost in the long cooking process of canning. According to Jean Carper in her book *Food—Your Miracle Medicine* (HarperCollins, 1993), we should eat both raw and cooked vegetables, but the vegetables should be *lightly* cooked (not stewed or boiled). Eating canned fruits and vegetables occasionally won't hurt us, however, and can be a welcome financial boost. I have found that canned vegetables and fruits are sometimes cheaper than fresh or frozen versions.

Don't forget that fruit and vegetable juices can help us reach our five-a-day goal too. These are helpful in the winter months when there is less variety of fresh produce available. Fruit juice in the morning and a mixed vegetable juice as a snack are very healthy.

Cooking Tip: A good way to cook vegetables is in the microwave—with only a teaspoon of water or none at all. All of the nutrients stay in the vegetables and they retain a good texture and color.

SPECIALTY FOOD ITEMS

With the health craze increasing the consumption of low-fat and low-cholesterol foods, we sometimes think we have to buy these items in order to eat healthily. We need to keep this in perspective. (We also must remember that just because something is fat-free doesn't always mean it's good for you.) The marketing folks at the food manufacturers know this too. Have you noticed the re-labeling on many foods? Hershey's chocolate syrup now claims to be fat-free. (It always has been.) Again, all we need to do is learn to cook with less of the bad fats. Here are some tips I have learned to make low-fat treats.

Fat Substitute Chart	
To lower the fat content in:	Replace the oil in the recipe with equal amounts of:
cakes, cookies, and breads	applesauce
chocolate cake, cookies, brownies	pureed prunes (baby food works well)
sauces and dressings	nonfat yogurt
mayonnaise or sour cream	nonfat yogurt

LUNCHES

Many folks struggle with how to provide a healthy lunch for the kids (or hubby) that can travel in a lunchbox. Whenever I need to pack a lunch, I try one of the ideas listed below. Whether you use these ideas or others, try to include the following several times per week: fruits, vegetables, grain products (especially whole-grain types), lean meat or alternates (dry beans, peas, lentils, peanuts, and eggs), and low-fat milk, cheese, or yogurt.

Main Dishes

- tuna fish sandwich
- egg salad
- ants on a log (celery stick with peanut butter and raisins on top)
- bagel and cream cheese
- lunch-meat sandwich
- peanut butter and jelly sandwich
- soup with crackers or corn bread
- cold pasta salad with whatever you like (olives, cheese chunks, celery, tofu pieces)
- leftovers
- black-bean spread on whole-wheat bread
- tortilla rolled up with shredded carrot and a turkey slice
- burritos
- risotto mixed with vegetables, and a green salad
- cheese enchiladas and rice
- tofu stir-fry and fresh fruit
- chicken salad with crackers
- homemade pizza and breadsticks
- cold barbecued chicken
- cheese and crackers and fresh fruit
- hamburger
- hot dog
- sloppy joes (pack bun separately)
- baked beans
- spaghetti or goulash
- stir-fry with rice

Snacks

- homemade granola bars
- muffins
- homemade cookies
- carrot or celery sticks
- homemade pudding, gelatin, or rice pudding
- fruit
- applesauce
- zucchini or banana bread
- graham crackers
- pudding
- snack mix (pretzels, unsalted peanuts, raisins, sunflower seeds)
- popcorn with spices (chili powder, taco seasoning, Lawry's seasoning, cheese powder)
- dips: pretzel sticks and peanut butter; apple slices and peanut butter; breadsticks and low-fat Cheez Whiz; tortilla chips and salsa; vegetables and ranch dressing

The key is to pack these in your own containers and not buy the prepackaged individual-sized servings. Invest in containers to keep hot foods warm and an insulated lunchbox or bag to keep cold things cold.

Drinks

Buy a small reusable bottle and fill it with juice, homemade lemonade, or milk. Avoid the prepackaged juice boxes or small cans. They cost twice as much as filling a reusable bottle from a larger juice container. Make your own juice from frozen concentrate and save up to three times the cost. This is true even when comparing name-brand frozen juice to its prepared and bottled equal. Make lunchbox juices by reusing small water bottles and filling with juice.

Avoid ades or punches; these just add sugar water to your

drink and cost too much. Stick to 100 percent fruit juices. Try making your own drinks: vegetable juice and fruit juice mixed (equal parts of orange and tomato juice) or fruit juice cooler (unsweetened fruit juice and club soda).

Lunchbox Tips to Make It Work

Invest in a small freezer pack that can keep any perishable dish cold. Or instead of buying an ice pack, fill a water bottle. Freeze it the night before and pack it with the lunch in the morning. It will be thawed enough to drink at lunchtime and keeps the food cold.

Leftover Tip

If you make enough at dinnertime to have leftovers, but your family eats everything you put on the table, try this tip. After the meal is made, but before you serve it, set aside enough for lunches. What they don't see they won't miss. Leftover lunches can save up to two thousand dollars per year.

Burritos and More

Make inexpensive burritos by layering refried beans, Spanish rice, and cheese on flour tortillas. Make your own Spanish rice by mixing rice with some seasoned canned tomatoes. Avoid instant rice; it costs more. Buy the flour tortillas, refried beans, and cheese in bulk. You can make thirty or more burritos in assembly-line fashion in little time. Wrap each one in plastic wrap and freeze. They make a great snack or lunchbox idea. If a microwave isn't available to reheat an item, warm it in the morning and pack it with a warmed insulating wrap or in an insulated lunch bag.

You can also freeze hot dogs, hamburgers, and breakfast sandwiches/burritos. Peanut butter and jelly sandwiches freeze well. Make several and freeze in small plastic bags. Hot dogs and hamburgers will taste best if grilled first (make a large batch). Freeze in a bun and warm to eat. The breakfast sandwich can be made ahead of time by combining a fried egg, a slice of American cheese, and a slice of ham with an English muffin. Wrap up tightly and freeze. Reheat when ready to eat.

Make It Appealing

Kids like small things. You can make their lunchbox goodies more appealing: cookies can be cut with smaller cookie cutters; brownies can be baked in mini-muffin tins. Cut sandwiches into four pieces. Use tiny plastic boxes to make it fun. This one-time purchase of a couple tiny boxes can be reused all year.

Bread Boredom

Are they bored with the same old bread? Try these different types to zip things up: cinnamon bread, French bread, multigrain bread, raisin bread, cheese bread, rye bread, oatmeal bread, Boston brown bread, pumpernickel bread, herb bread, onion bread, potato bread, bran bread, pitas, hot

BREAD MACHINES

I compared the cost of store-bought loaves of plain white, whole wheat, and buttermilk bread with equivalent loaves baked in a bread machine. The cost was about the same. Only multigrain bread was cheaper when made in a bread machine.

If the multigrain loaf contained several types of grains, a store-bought multigrain loaf of comparable size would cost about $4.50. A homemade loaf of equal size and grain usage would cost about $1.50.

I don't often recommend buying a bread machine because most people don't use it much, or they usually make white bread. Also, the initial purchase price is high. But often we just want the scrumptious taste of warm, freshly baked bread. If you can afford the expense of the machine for this purpose alone, then go for it.

dog buns, English muffins, sub rolls, hamburger buns, kaiser rolls, bagels, hard rolls, biscuits, tortillas, rice cakes, or crackers.

Nutrition

I have heard from many moms that they feel they need to purchase prepackaged lunchbox meals in order to provide healthier low-fat foods, and that being frugal and making the lunches means eating high-fat or high-starch meals. I want to take a minute to discuss this myth.

Making a homemade lunch doesn't mean it has to be high in fat or starch. Often you can replace the same item for a low-fat version. For example, buy chicken or turkey hot dogs instead of full beef, or buy the more expensive fat-free ones if you can. For macaroni and cheese, replace the milk with low-fat or nonfat milk and the butter with yogurt. For bagels and cream cheese, buy low-fat or nonfat cream cheese. Peanut butter is high in fat but also high in protein. You don't need too much to meet a person's protein needs. Try all-natural peanut butter with no added oil or sugar. For the tuna and egg salads, you can replace the mayonnaise with low-fat or nonfat mayonnaise or yogurt. Disguising the taste with relish is helpful. Ham lunch meat is usually as low in fat as turkey and can often be purchased more cheaply on sale or in bulk from warehouse clubs.

Snack foods don't have to be bread-based. They can be sliced vegetables, fruit, or even a fruit or green salad (with dressing on the side so it won't get soggy). The low-fat and nonfat versions of mayonnaise, yogurt, milk, salad dressings, etc., are not that different in price and can be bought on sale in the same manner as other items.

Staying within budget and keeping it healthy at lunch takes

the same planning and forethought as other meals. You can do it.

Resources

For resources on vegetarian cooking, see the Resource section in chapter 10, "Cut Back on Meats."

Better Than Store-Bought, Elizabeth Witty (Harper Collins, 1985).

Cheaper and Better: Homemade Alternatives to Store-Bought Goods, Nancy Birnes (Harper & Row Publishers, 1988), out of print; check library for copy.

Eat Healthy for $50 a Week: Feed Your Family Nutritious Delicious Meals for Less, Rhonda Barfield (Kensington Publishing, 1996).

Make-a-Mix, Karine Eliason (Fisher Books, 1995).

Make Your Own Groceries, Daphne Hartwig (Bobbs-Merrill, 1983), out of print; check library for copy.

More-With-Less Cookbook, Doris J. Longacre (Herald Press, 2000).

Not Just Beans: 50 Years of Frugal Family Favorites, Tawra J. Kellam (Not Just Beans, 1999).

The Use-It-Up Cookbook: A Guide for Minimizing Food Waste, Lois C. Willand (Practical Cookbooks, 1979).

Will It Freeze? An A to Z Guide to Foods That Freeze, Joan Hood (Charles Scribner's Sons, 1982), out of print; check library for copy.

GUIDELINE 7:

Eliminate Convenience Foods

Convenience foods have eaten up (no pun intended) many of my grocery dollars in the past. I have shopped when hungry, looked at those yummy-looking packages that say, "You can eat me now—without the fuss," and taken them home. I have smelled and tasted the samples available during peak shopping hours—and bought the item.

Convenience foods are just that—convenient. And you are going to pay for that convenience, sometimes more than you think. With some planning, you can make your own meals and snacks from scratch, and you'll cut way back on your food bill. In my price studies, this is what I've found about the cost of convenience foods:

- A restaurant meal costs six to ten times more than one made from scratch.

- A frozen meal costs four times more than one made from scratch.

- A prepackaged mix costs three times more than one made from scratch.

- Precut foods (ready-to-eat salads, sliced carrots, shredded cheese) cost two times more than if you cut them yourself.

One of my favorite examples of paying for convenience comes from a woman who called asking for help with her budget. She had no idea why she was always short of money at the end of the month. After much discussion, we figured it out. Every morning on her way to work she stopped at Starbucks for a cup of coffee and a muffin. She didn't think it added up to anything, but we calculated that she was spending a hundred dollars per month for that convenience.

By changing your lifestyle a bit, you can save a great deal. To get away from the need for convenience foods, there are a number of things you can do. The first is to *plan* your meals so the fancy packages and smells in the store don't influence you. Have a meal plan and specific shopping list and buy only what is on your list. And make sure you aren't hungry when you shop!

The second thing you need to do is become comfortable with your *kitchen* (you know, that room with the refrigerator in it). Plan on spending a little more time there and learn to cook some things from scratch. When I was a guest on *The Gayle King Show,* I made a sample shopping list for a guest. One item on the list was a block of cheese (instead of presliced cheese at the deli counter, which would cost her $1.50 more *per pound*). Gayle asked, "But what do you do if you want a slice of cheese?" I told her she would have to take a knife and slice it! It's amazing how people have grown accustomed to pre-sliced and pre-chopped foods.

Third, but certainly not least, is to buy items you use often in *bulk.* This helps avoid the convenience items when you run out of your stock and rush to the store to get whatever will work in its place (but at a higher cost). If time is a problem for you, then cooking several meals ahead of time would be advantageous. I talk more about this later in the book, but I wanted to mention some important tips about cooking in advance. By doubling recipes and freezing half for another day, I am able to build up a reserve of meals in the freezer. This is homemade convenience food. You pull out a meal and stick it in the microwave or oven—just like the one that is four times more expensive in the pretty box.

Having meals in the freezer also keeps us from being tempted by those costly last-minute meals. I often used to order a pizza (twenty dollars) when I was too tired to cook or didn't have time to thaw the meat or cook from scratch. Now I have a frozen meal conveniently waiting on days like that.

Eating out is something we also did when I was tired. But that really adds up quickly. The average American family eats out four times per week, including dinners, lunches, and brunches. The national average for money spent eating out is eighty-five dollars per week per family.

Even meals made at home using pre-made mixes, sauces, etc., are costly. The take-and-bake pizzas are cheaper than a baked and delivered one, but they are still four or five times more expensive than homemade. Let's compare a chicken-and-noodle dinner for one person made from scratch, a box mix, a frozen pre-made meal, and eating out:

- from scratch: $2.50
- a box mix: $3.99
- frozen pre-made: $4.50
- eating out: $7.99

That's a savings of $5.50 for this meal alone. If most meals have this type of cost variation, think of the difference you can make over a month's time (ninety meals). You could save up to five hundred dollars a month!

The marketing of prepackaged mixes is deceptive as well. Many ads lead us to believe we are making a home-cooked meal when we use their package. This sly marketing ploy appeals to your instinct that homemade is better (and cheaper). Remember, if the manufacturer did anything to "help" you make it, you are paying them for that help.

CHAPTER 10

GUIDELINE 8:

Cut Back on Meats

This chapter may sound extreme to some readers. Eating meatless meals is a big step to take. Remember, this was one more way we found to save money. If it's too extreme, move on to the next guideline. Or try these ideas once in a while to help the budget a bit. Some people have mentioned that eating frugally shouldn't have to mean eating beans and tofu. It doesn't have to, but including them is the cheapest way. You'll never find meat for forty cents per pound, but there is a meat alternative that cooks up like beef at that price. If meat is a must in your home, skip this chapter and just incorporate my tips in chapter 8, "Make Your Own Whenever Possible," on reducing *some* of your meat expenses.

I had two reasons for reducing the meat in my diet. My first was a monetary reason. Meats are a very expensive source of protein. Dried beans are an excellent source of protein, carbohydrates, iron, thiamin, and fiber. They cost very little—usually one-tenth the cost of meat. They can be added to many types of dishes and are filling as well.

My second reason for reducing meat in our diet was health. I knew we needed protein, but I knew there were more nutritious sources of protein. I also knew we ate more protein than we needed. Most adult Americans eat too much protein. Even though the recommended serving size is three ounces, the average serving for dinner is between eight and ten ounces of meat. Unless you are a growing child or pregnant, you probably need about half that amount. But a plate looks a bit empty with a small cut of meat or chicken on it.

We are supposed to eat more vegetables and fruit than most of us are eating. Only 20 percent of Americans eat the recommended minimum serving of fruits and vegetables (five per day). By reducing our meat and stretching it with more vegetables and fruits, we can solve two problems at once. Dishes like stir-fry, fajitas, salads, stews, potpies, and casseroles call for many vegetables and grains with a smaller amount of meat. These cost less to prepare and are more nutritious. I also added more alternative proteins (dried beans, tofu, grains) to our diet. There are some very healthy meatless dishes that our family enjoys.

When I first cut down on meat, I wanted to make sure we were getting the protein and other nutrients we needed. I started my nutrient research with protein. I wanted enough, but not too much, since extra protein turns into fat.

I looked at the recommended daily needs for protein for each member of our family (available in most nutrition books) and added up the foods we usually ate to see if we were getting what we needed. We were—and had some to spare. The average adult needs 60 grams of protein per day. The Recommended Dietary Allowance for protein is .80 grams per kilogram of body weight, or .36 grams per pound of body weight. So a 120-pound person would need 44 grams of protein, and a 180-pound person would need 65 grams of protein. People's need for protein increases (as much as three times) if they are ill, under stress, pregnant, or nursing. Please consult a doctor before altering your diet.

I researched the types of proteins that provide the most

protein per pound while still watching fat intake. Here is what I found:

Proteins in Food			
Food Item	Quantity	Protein	Fat
Hamburger, 17% fat (lean)	3 oz.	21 gm.	17 gm.
Chicken breast, skinless	3 oz.	27 gm.	4 gm.
Chicken dark meat, skinless	3 oz.	27 gm.	6 gm.
Turkey breast, skinless	3 oz.	27 gm.	9 gm.
Cod (and most fish)	3 oz.	28 gm.	5 gm.
Tuna	3 oz.	8 gm.	7 gm.
Egg	1	6 gm.	4 gm.
Yogurt, nonfat	1 C.	8 gm.	0 gm.
Milk, nonfat	1 C.	8 gm.	0 gm.
Peanut butter	1 T.	4 gm.	8 gm.
Peanuts	½ C.	18 gm.	25 gm.
Hot dog	1	5 gm.	13 gm.
Brown rice	1 C. cooked	5 gm.	1 gm.
Tofu	4 oz.	10 gm.	4 gm.
Dried beans, lentils	1 C.	15 gm.	0 gm.

By looking at these figures, I realized we easily meet our protein needs. Meats could be served less frequently. Most countries use meat as flavoring or to enhance a dish. Their plates are two-thirds filled with grains, vegetables, or fruit. Americans tend to feature the meat, and the rest is considered a "side dish." In light of the nutritional information we are hearing, we need more vegetables and whole grains—so the rebalancing of our plates seems not only better for us but also for our wallets.

I began serving smaller portions of meat at mealtimes, filling the plate with grains, vegetables, and fruits. I stretched the meat in dishes such as stir-fry, fajitas, rice and beans, etc. I sometimes tried meatless recipes. You can feed a family either a steak dinner or lentil soup with whole grain rolls, and they will get the same amount of protein. But they won't cost the same.

Make sure your family is getting the complete protein they need from a meatless dish. A complete protein is the end result of two incomplete amino acids combining to form a complete protein. For example, brown rice is an incomplete protein, and beans are an incomplete protein, but when combined, they make a complete protein. Other examples of complete protein combinations are listed below.

According to nutrition experts, the key to making the combinations complete is making sure the grains are *whole* grains. Dr. Mauro Di Pasquale, Olympic medical committee member and author of *Amino Acids and Proteins for the Athlete* (CRC Press, 1997), states that we need to combine *whole* grains to make a complete protein combination. In other words, if we combine *white* rice with beans, it is not a complete protein—it needs to be brown rice. The same goes for whole-wheat breads: They need to be 100 percent *whole*-grain breads. Many manufacturers take out much of the wheat and replace a portion of it to add fiber or color, but we need the entire kernel. Make sure the ingredient list includes 100 percent whole wheat flour. If it simply says "whole-wheat flour," it may, in fact, be only part of the wheat.

If you want to try a few meatless dishes, here are some guidelines to make sure you are getting the right combinations to form a complete protein.

Complete Protein Combinations		
whole grains	+	legumes
whole grains	+	dairy
legumes	+	nuts or seeds
legumes	+	dairy
vegetables	+	legumes

Legumes are defined as plants that have pods with rows of seeds inside. Some examples are chickpeas, beans (kidney, lima, garbanzo, etc.), lentils, peanuts, and alfalfa.

Whole grains are amaranth, quinoa (pronounced KEEN-wa), millet, buckwheat, rice, rye, oats, wheat, barley, spelt, and corn.

Please note that nuts and grains do not form a complete protein. Also note that peanuts are legumes, not nuts.

Here are some example dishes we eat that use the above combinations:

Whole Grains + Legumes

lentil and brown rice casserole
brown rice and beans
whole-grain pita bread and hummus
baked beans and brown (whole-grain) bread
black-eyed peas and brown rice
peanut butter and jelly on whole-grain bread
corn and lima beans (succotash)
refried beans on whole-grain tortilla
falafel
corn bread and pinto beans
bean burrito on a corn tortilla
oat muffins and soy milk

Whole Grains + Dairy

brown rice and cheese
whole-wheat bread and cheese
oatmeal and milk
whole-wheat macaroni and cheese
whole-wheat pizza with cheese

Legumes + Nuts

cashew and peanut butter sandwich
bean and walnut salad
lentil and nut loaf

Legumes + Dairy

beans and cheese
refried beans with cheese
lentil soup with yogurt
yogurt with peanuts

Vegetables + Legumes

bean and vegetable soup
eggplant and lentil casserole

How close together must foods be eaten to complement each other? From what I've read, most experts say complementary proteins don't have to be consumed in the same meal but can be eaten within a few hours of each other on the same day.

My newfound zest for alternate sources of protein did not, however, cause me to become a complete vegetarian. Legumes and grains are a great source of most complete proteins, but some nutritionists teach that these combinations leave other elements lacking that can only be found in certain dairy, egg, or meat products. Some of these elements are choline, vitamin B_{12}, and vitamin D. This is why many legume dishes are combined with a small portion of cheese, meat, or eggs. If a person never eats an occasional meat, egg, dairy, or fish dish, some nutritionists suggest they might be deficient in these elements. I am not an expert on diet and am merely sharing my findings. I suggest you discuss these issues with a licensed dietitian before changing your diet, and do some research on your own. Some books on the topic are listed at the end of this chapter. Beans and tofu are an excellent way to stretch the budget. There are also some meatless recipes in chapter 15, "Some Great Recipes."

TOFU AND SOYBEAN PRODUCTS

Products made from the legume soybean (tofu, TVP, soy milk, and tempeh) are complete proteins and do not need to be combined with grains. They have zero cholesterol and are very inexpensive. They make a great money-saving meatless meal.

Soy products contain trace elements not found in any other plant. One example is choline, an essential element to the body. So far, it is found only in eggs, liver, and soybeans. Anyone avoiding all animal proteins should learn to incorporate tofu or other soybean products into their diet in order to be well balanced.

TVP stands for texturized vegetable protein, a food product made from soy flour. It comes in a dried form and needs to be hydrated. It can be bought from local health food stores in several sizes, including granules (like ground beef), chunks (like chicken chunks), and patties (like chicken breasts). It has no flavor, so it needs to be seasoned. One half cup of dried TVP plus a half cup of hot water converts into one cup of a ready-to-use hamburger-like ingredient. It costs about forty cents per

DRIED BEAN PREPARATION TIPS

One cup of dried beans will expand into two and a half cups after cooking.

Freeze in meal-sized bags. You can then drop the frozen bean portion into the cooking dish or soup. They will have a similar texture to canned beans.

Soak beans before cooking to reduce cooking time and the amount of carbohydrates in the beans, which causes gas. There are two methods for soaking beans before cooking. In both methods, first rinse the beans and remove any beans that float.

The overnight method: Cover the beans with cold water (four cups water to one cup beans) and let sit overnight. Drain, cover with water, and boil as directed.

The quick-soak method: Place the beans in a pot, cover with water, then boil for ten minutes. Remove from heat and keep covered. Allow to stand for one hour. Drain and rinse beans. Continue with your recipe.

Cooking times vary depending on the type of beans you are using.

white (or navy) beans and soybeans—up to four hours
larger beans—two to three hours
smaller beans—one hour
lentils—one and a half hours
lima beans—up to one and a half hours

---

pound when hydrated. Once hydrated, use it as you would its meat equivalent. A great source of recipes for its use is *The TVP Cookbook* by Dorothy Bates.

Tofu can also be very inexpensive (99¢ to $2.59 per pound). It is even less expensive if you buy it directly from Asian grocery stores.

Tofu is very bland and can be incorporated into any dish. We have made custard with soft tofu and used firm tofu in spaghetti sauces, sandwiches, stir-fries, and casseroles in place of meat. It can be mixed with flour and spices to form a burger patty. Soft tofu can also replace any recipe that calls for cottage cheese, ricotta, or yogurt. When frozen and then thawed, tofu has the texture of ground beef. It takes on the flavor of whatever you add to it and is low in fat. The firmer the texture of the tofu, the higher the protein content. It has the same amount of calcium as milk. Most supermarkets carry it, making it easy to incorporate into your menus.

--------------------  --------------------

This Can't Be Tofu! 75 Recipes to Cook Something You Never Thought You Would—and Love Every Bite, Deborah Madison (Bantam Publishing, 2000).

The TVP Cookbook, Dorothy Bates (The Book Publishing Company, 1991).

The Vegetarian Way, Virginia Messina, MPH, RD, and Mark Messina, PhD (Harmony Books, 1996).

CHAPTER 11

GUIDELINE 9:

Waste Nothing

The "waste nothing" mentality was more common in previous generations than it is now. Nothing was thrown out until it had been so used or recycled that it became useless for anything more. Defining when something becomes useless varies from home to home.

Our grandparents were creative in finding uses for almost everything that came into their hands. Flour sacks were converted into dish towels and dresses for the girls. (I even have an antique quilt hanging in my home that is filled with small squares of material from those flour sacks.) Jars were reused to store homemade foods or small tools or nails. Food that would be thrown out was fed to animals. Wood from broken crates was converted into furniture or toys. Old tires were cut and used to resole shoes. The list could go on and on because there was no end to their creativity and resourcefulness in recycling.

We are being raised in a "disposable" age. Our parents wanted us to have it easier than they did, but with this blessing we lost an art. We don't know how to stretch things. We expect things to be ready-made, and then we throw them out when we're done with them. But this generation is learning there must be a better way; we can stretch things a bit further. We recycle our cans and plastics to avoid filling up the landfills needlessly. We reuse large food containers for storing dry goods or small toys. Oatmeal containers make good small-toy storage or a toy in itself (see chapter 29, "Crafts for Kids"). The large laundry detergent jugs can be used to store baking mixes (wash very well first). Milk cartons can be used for bird feeders or freezer containers. See additional reuse ideas in chapter 7, "Buy in Bulk Whenever Possible."

We can apply this "reuse" mentality to our food as well. Many leftovers can be made into another meal. The ends of bread loaves can be saved in the freezer for croutons, stuffing, bread pudding, or bread crumbs. Fruit about to turn extra ripe can be made into smoothie drinks, pudding, Popsicles, jam, or fruit breads. Bananas can be frozen in their skins until needed for baking. Bits of vegetables and meats can go into a pot in the freezer to be used in soups, stews, potpies, enchiladas, or stir-fry meals. Soak limp celery in ice water for several hours to revitalize it or chop and freeze it for use in casseroles.

My favorite book on the subject of reusing foods is the *Use-It-Up Cookbook* by Lois Willand. It lists every food you may encounter in alphabetical order. Each section lists uses for that food, recipes, and storage tips. It is very valuable for stretching food.

There is no end to the ways we can recycle wisely. And there are many creative people out there who can teach us new ways to reuse items. If you would like some more creative ideas for reusing items, please visit your local library.

-------------------------- *Resources* --------------------------

Don't Throw It Out: Recycle, Renew and Reuse to Make Things Last,
   Lori Baird (Rodale Press, 2007).

Living More With Less, Doris Longacre (Herald Press, 2003).

*Reduce, Reuse, Recycle: An Easy Household Guide (The Chelsea
   Green Guides),* Nicky Scott (Chelsea Green Publishing, 2005).

GUIDELINE 10:

Institute a Soup-and-Bread or Baked-Potato Night

Having soup and bread for dinner once each week helps us stay within our food budget. Soups are inexpensive to make (when made from scratch), and they are nutritious. There are such a variety of soups in the world; you could try a new one every week and never repeat a soup recipe all year. Each country has some well-known soups in its cuisine. They probably have soup often for the same reason we do—it's inexpensive.

Most soups contain vegetables, some stock, a protein source (meat, fish, tofu, TVP), and a starch of some type (potato, noodles, rice, etc.). These are the ingredients for a healthy meal. Check in your cookbooks for some recipes to get you started. There are cold soups, spicy soups, thick ones, and thin ones. Just about anything your family likes can be found in a soup form.

I avoid soup mixes and canned soups because of the high costs as well as the fact that they are not as nutritious as homemade soups. The canned and dried mixes have been cooked to death, highly salted, and loaded with additives to keep them "fresh" for you. Soup and bread made from scratch usually costs me two to three dollars for the four of us. The same meal made from canned soup and store-bought bread or ready-to-bake biscuits would run nine dollars. To keep the cost down, I use leftover meat and vegetables that couldn't be used for anything else. I keep a bowl in the freezer for these leftovers. When the bowl is full, I can make soup or a stir-fry dish. Things that I might put in the bowl are a leg of chicken that isn't enough for a lunch, vegetables left in the pan after dinner, or vegetables that will spoil if not used right away. Anything is usable for a stew or soup. This is originally what soups and stews were—leftovers stretched into one more meal. If time is a real problem for you, try making your own instant soup mix and having it ready for dinnertime. I have included some ideas in this chapter on how to make a soup mix.

The type of bread I like to serve with my soups is usually homemade biscuits. I serve corn bread once in a while for variety. And I bake bread if I have time. But there are so many simple biscuit recipes in cookbooks that take almost no time to mix and bake. For biscuit variety, add sour cream or yogurt instead of milk to make them fluffier. Add grated cheese to make them richer. Add herbs (dill or thyme) to make them tastier. Be creative. For those with time constraints, make up a master baking mix (most cookbooks have one—mine is in chapter 8, "Make Your Own Whenever Possible"). With these, all you need to do at dinner is add shortening and milk. If you really hate to mix up biscuits, the only cheap alternative I have seen is the canned refrigerator rolls that go on sale for about seventy-five cents per can. They are full of preservatives but are a quick solution.

My kids were not excited about the idea of soup night. Yours may not be either. Start them with something you think they'll like, such as a potato and cheese soup. When it's blended together, it's rich and cheesy. If they like wontons, try a wonton soup. If they like beans, try a black bean soup. If they like noodles, try chicken noodle soup. If they like lentils, make lentil soup. Start slow. Kids will adapt if they know that's all there is for dinner.

To help you get started, some of my favorite soup recipes are listed below.

BAKED-POTATO NIGHT

If soup is absolutely out of the question, try a baked potato night. Potatoes go on sale regularly for forty cents per pound (a five-pound bag for two dollars). Save the same leftovers in the freezer, but serve them as potato toppers. Add some grated cheese, diced tomatoes, diced leftover chicken, diced vegetables, and onions to the smorgasbord. Or take a baked potato, scoop out the center, mix the center with ground beef and taco spices, and re-stuff the potato. Potato night is another cheap meal that can be done instead of soup night.

SOUP RECIPES

Instant Cream Soup Mix

2 C. nonfat dry milk
¾ C. cornstarch
¼ C. instant chicken bouillon
1 tsp. onion powder
½ tsp. dried thyme
½ tsp. dried basil
¼ tsp. pepper

Combine these ingredients and store in an airtight container.

To use for soup, combine ⅓ cup of the mix and 1½ cups of water. Bring to a boil while stirring often. Add a vegetable for more flavor or texture, such as diced celery (for cream of celery soup), sliced mushrooms (for cream of mushroom soup), or diced broccoli (for cream of broccoli soup).

To use in any recipe calling for a can of cream of mushroom, chicken, or celery soup, add ¹/₃ cup of the mix to 1¼ cups of water. Boil for a few minutes, stirring often.

Quick Potato-Cheese Soup

1 T. butter
1 onion, diced
2 T. flour
1 tsp. salt
1 tsp. pepper
1 C. water
1 C. leftover mashed potatoes   ·
2 C. milk
½ C. grated cheese

In a saucepan, melt butter and sauté the onion until light brown. Stir in the flour and salt and pepper. Stir, forming a roux paste. Add water, stirring constantly. When mixed, add the rest of the ingredients. Stir while it thickens and the cheese melts.

Tip: You can replace the potato in most recipes with a turnip, if desired. They require the same cooking time and have a similar texture.

Black Bean Soup

2 (15 oz.) cans black beans or 2 C. prepared beans
1 (15 oz.) can stewed tomatoes
1 (14.5 oz.) can chicken broth
1 onion, chopped
1 garlic clove, crushed
salt and pepper to taste
1 T. oregano
2 T. lime juice

Combine ingredients (except lime juice) in a large pan and simmer until throughly heated. Add the lime juice after the soup is cooked. Serve with homemade rolls or rice.

My Mom's Best Pea Soup

(Note: This isn't split-pea soup)

> 2½ C. chicken broth
> 1 12-oz. package frozen peas, thawed or 1 cup cooked fresh peas
> 1 tsp. tarragon
> 1 tsp. salt
> 1 tsp. pepper
> 1 T. butter
> 1 T. flour
> 2 T. lemon juice
> 1 C. milk

Put broth, peas, and spices in a blender and blend until fairly smooth. It will be a bit chunky. In a pan, melt butter and add flour to form a paste. Pour the blender contents into the pan and bring to a boil. Boil, stirring occasionally, for ten minutes. Remove from heat and add lemon juice and milk.

CHAPTER 13

GUIDELINE 11:

Cook Several Meals at Once and Freeze Them

There have been many excellent books written on cooking and freezing meals in advance. Two of my favorite books on the subject are *Frozen Assets—How to Cook for a Day and Eat for a Month* by Deborah Taylor-Hough, and *Mega Cooking* by Jill Bond.

Both authors teach you how the system works. These ladies do a good job of explaining the whole concept of cooking monthly, and they give you several sample menus and recipes to follow. Jill Bond also shows you how to convert your recipes into any bulk cooking plan—whether you want to cook for four or forty!

Both books share the same premise—the more you cook in bulk, the more you'll save. Both books explain how shopping and cooking in bulk will save you money and time in the kitchen. It takes between two and three days to do all of the shopping, food preparation, and cooking for thirty days. With both plans, you are shopping and preparing food up to the baking stage. For the evening meal, you merely thaw and bake the meal. A few dishes are precooked and only require reheating. Both books also offer many recipes.

Preparing meals in advance saves you money in several

ways. It will reduce your grocery bill and energy bill and will save you time. The grocery bill will be less because you are able to buy foods in bulk. A five-pound package of hamburger or a ten-pound bag of potatoes is cheaper than buying the same in lesser quantities. You also will spend less since you will be in the store less often, and you won't pick up those impulse items each time you walk down the aisles.

Having meals in the freezer also saves by reducing the impulse to eat out or to order a pizza. When you are running late, you are too tired to cook, or the family is complaining that there is nothing to eat, you can say, "Dinner's in the freezer." This can be very handy for busy families.

You also save energy costs by cooking in bulk. Cooking several items at once doesn't require more energy than just one dish would and reduces the stove's use threefold. Browning ten pounds of hamburger instead of browning each pound separately saves time and energy.

As for your time in the kitchen, it will be reduced considerably. Most of us spend an hour in the kitchen getting dinner ready. If all of the chopping and mixing is done ahead of time, and all that is required is reheating or popping something into the oven, consider how much more free time you will have. Wouldn't it be nice if all of the celery and onions were diced at once?

I usually recommend that people try cooking in bulk gradually. It can be a bit overwhelming to plan a month of shopping and slicing. To start, just double or triple tonight's meal and freeze the extra. Do the same tomorrow. And in a few days you will have two to three weeks of meals stocked up with no extra sweat or planning. The reason I suggest the slow approach is to let you adjust to the idea of buying, cooking, and storing in bulk. If I sent you off to try a four-month plan now, I think you'd close this book and forget it. A four-month plan will save you the most money, but first you need to learn how to shop and plan ahead. Once you do, you will be ready to tackle larger amounts of planning and cooking.

STORAGE SPACE

People say they can't cook in bulk because they don't have the extra freezer space. As I've mentioned before, I got rid of my extra freezer years ago when I learned it was consuming a fair amount of money in electricity. Now I have only the small freezer above my refrigerator, but I have no difficulty freezing meals in this small space. I even store foods bought in bulk, such as hamburger and chicken. To expand my freezer space, I cleared out all unnecessary items to make room for important things. I asked myself if it would be used soon, how much it was saving me, and if it could it be stored in the refrigerator instead. I then went to a hardware store and purchased a wire rack shelf for three dollars that divided the freezer in half. This created more storage space.

My next step was to freeze in containers that used less space. Storing in large zippered freezer bags takes very little space. When filled with a meal and laid flat, they are only an inch or so thick. Ten can be stacked on top of each other, two stacks to a shelf. Plastic containers are too bulky to make my small space useful.

Some people have questioned the cost of my plastic-bag usage and wonder if I am using up my savings. But by using sales and coupons, I pay a few cents per bag. Many can be washed and reused. If I used plastic containers, it would cost me more than a few plastic bags.

FOOD SAFETY

One main concern when freezing in bulk is food handling and long-term freezing. Which foods are safe to freeze cooked or uncooked, and how long is it safe to freeze them? I found some wonderful resources on these topics and have listed them below.

- U.S. Department of Agriculture Food Safety
  www.fsis.usda.gov/Food_Safety_Education/index.asp

- Food and Drug Administration (FDA)
  http://vm.cfsan.fda.gov/list.html or 1-888-SAFEFOOD
  Information on foods, drugs, cosmetics, etc.

- Butterball Turkey Hotline
  www.butterball.com or 1-800-BUTTERBALL
  In November and December they will answer your turkey baking questions.

- Weber Grill Line
  www.weber.com or 1-800-GRILL-OUT
  During the summer months, staff are available Monday through Friday, and prerecorded messages are available 24 hours a day to answer grilling questions.

--------------------------  --------------------------

Dinner's In the Freezer, Jill Bond (Hibbard Publications, 2000).

Don't Panic—Dinner's in the Freezer: Great-Tasting Meals You Can Make Ahead, Susie Martinez, Vanda Howell, and Bonnie Garcia (Revell, 2005).

Frozen Assets Lite and Easy: Cook for a Day, Eat for a Month, Deborah Taylor-Hough (Sourcebooks, Inc., 2003).

Mega Cooking: A Revolutionary New Plan for Quantity Cooking, Jill Bond (Cumberland House Publishing, 2000).

Will It Freeze, An A to Z Guide to Foods That Freeze, Joan Hood (Scribner, 2002).

CHAPTER 14

Special Dietary Needs

There are many folks who have special needs in their diet as a result of allergies or a chemical reaction to the additives in foods.

Children in particular react to some of the more than five thousand additives in our foods. It's not surprising, since these additives are chemicals and not elements found in nature. Most additives are petroleum derivatives. Other people have allergies to items commonly found in prepared foods (such as corn or milk). In order to work around these elements, people must find alternatives to items normally purchased and taken for granted. For example, instead of buying the crackers (or whatever) that are on sale, some people must eat only specific name brands that are known to not have additives or a particular food ingredient. This can raise the price of your grocery bill.

We experienced this challenge a few years ago. Our son reacted to additives in food and in the air (perfumes, solvents, fumes, etc.). We needed to buy only foods that were additive-free. This did not mean I could only shop at health food stores; I found most of our needs at local stores. But it did mean that

I could no longer pick up the generic brand or the weekly special. This put a big crimp in our penny-pinching ways. This new challenge required an even deeper adherence to the eleven guidelines for a miserly way of life.

I have had several people express doubt that they can eat healthy and spend only half of what they usually spend for groceries. It can be done! When special needs must be taken into consideration, it takes even more planning and shopping than the average miserly mom does. You can't just drop in to a health food store with your shopping list and expect to save money. Our newest challenge in shopping helped prove to others that it can be done.

To keep within my grocery budget, I needed to plan even more carefully. I could never fall back on a convenience food or restaurant meal because my son couldn't eat the additives. This alone was an incentive to stay true to my guidelines. I could never say, "I'm too tired to cook from scratch" or "I'm too tired to shop." Just any brand of food was not an option. I had to watch all the local flyers for sales on the foods he could eat. I had to shop at several stores in order to buy the brands or types of foods within his dietary guidelines and still get them on sale. I used co-ops for the items only available at costly health food stores.

I made even more of our own foods than when I first started with the eleven guidelines. We ate less meat and poultry, replacing them with dried beans, whole grains, tofu, or TVP-based meals. This reduced our overall costs so I could afford the more expensive health food products. We applied all of the eleven guidelines a bit more than we had done before.

So when I hear people complain that it's too much work to save money, I think back to when we didn't have this additive problem. Reaching our financial goals was so much easier then.

But anyone can do it. There is help for this type of challenging cooking and shopping; agencies and support groups have researched the additive topic. If you want help or more information on allergies to food additives, contact the Feingold Association (800-321-3287, *www.feingold.org*). You would be amazed at the problems they have linked to additives: asthma, bed-wetting, aggression, sleeplessness, etc. They have cookbooks, shopping lists, and mail-order food addresses to help make this problem easier to manage.

Whatever your special dietary need, the eleven guidelines can help keep you within your budget. You might have to work harder than most or be a little more creative, but they will prove helpful for any situation.

Resources

Why Can't My Child Behave? Jane Hersey (Pear Tree Press, 1996).

Why Your Child Is Hyperactive, Ben F. Feingold, MD (Random House, 1985).

CHAPTER 15

Some Great Recipes

To supplement chapter 8, "Make Your Own Whenever Possible," I have included a selection of helpful recipes. (For more recipes, please look for my new cookbook, *Healthy Meals for Less*.) These are good in terms of flavor and nutrition as well as providing savings. After each recipe, I have provided a cost comparison analysis to show what the homemade version is saving you. My cost is based on my price goals.

BREAKFAST IDEAS

Pancakes

These are a great savings over cereal. The cheapest and tastiest recipe I have found is this one. To save time and energy, bake twice the amount you need and freeze the extras. They reheat well in the toaster or microwave.

2 eggs
2½ C. buttermilk or sour milk
1 tsp. baking soda
2½ C. flour

2 tsp. sugar
4 tsp. melted butter or vegetable oil
1 T. baking powder
1 tsp. salt

Beat all ingredients together until smooth. Spoon onto greased hot griddle. Flip over when bubbles appear.

Cost Analysis (one dozen):
Homemade = 50¢
Purchased Mix = $1.15
Frozen Microwave = $2.29

Maple-Flavored Syrup

2 C. sugar
1 C. water
1 tsp. maple extract

Bring water and sugar to a slow boil over low heat, stirring constantly. Remove from heat before it comes to a rolling boil (to keep crystals from forming). Add flavoring as it is cooling. Store in the refrigerator.

For thicker syrup, replace half of the water with corn syrup. You may also add butter flavoring purchased from the store. But both of these will increase the cost.

Cost Analysis (24 oz.):
Homemade = 30¢
Store-bought = $4.20

Cinnamon Rolls

These taste like the famous cinnamon rolls sold in malls.

Dough
1 T. dry yeast

1 C. warm milk
⅓ C. sugar
½ C. soft butter
1 tsp. salt
2 eggs
4 C. flour

Dissolve yeast in warm milk. Add the rest of the ingredients and mix well. Knead into a ball or put in a bread machine on the dough setting. Let rise until double in size. When ready, roll out to about ¼-inch thick. Spread with filling (recipe following).

Filling
¼ C. soft butter
1 C. brown sugar
3 T. cinnamon

Spread butter evenly on dough. Sprinkle sugar and cinnamon evenly over buttered dough. Roll up dough. Slice roll into 1-inch slices. Place on a greased pan. Let rise until double in size. Bake 10 minutes at 400°.

Icing
½ C. soft butter
1½ C. powdered sugar
1 oz. cream cheese
2 T. whipping cream
1 tsp. vanilla extract
pinch of salt

Combine all ingredients. Beat until fluffy. When rolls are hot, spread lots of icing on them.

Cost Analysis (per roll) (makes 16 to 18 rolls):
Homemade = 45¢
Store-bought = $3.99

Nonfat Granola

This is my husband's favorite breakfast cereal!

¾ C. brown sugar
⅓ C. concentrated apple juice from frozen concentrate
½ C. nonfat dry milk
⅓ C. honey
5 C. quick-cooking oats
2 T. cinnamon
½ tsp. salt
½ C. dried fruit

Mix sugar, juice, dry milk, and honey in saucepan and heat over medium heat only until sugar dissolves. Combine dry ingredients and fruit in mixing bowl. Pour sugar mixture slowly over dry mixture and blend well. Place on cookie sheet and bake at 375° for 10 to 20 minutes, stirring every 10 minutes.

Options: Be creative by adding peanuts, sunflower seeds, coconut, sesame seeds, peanut butter, or whatever else your family enjoys.

Cost Analysis (1 pound):
Homemade = $1.50
Store-bought = $3.29

SNACKS, BREADS, AND DRINKS

Chocolate Syrup (aka Hershey's Chocolate Syrup)

1 C. cocoa powder (unsweetened)
2 C. sugar
¼ tsp. salt
1 C. cold water
1 T. vanilla

Combine cocoa and sugar and blend until all lumps of cocoa

are gone. Add salt and water and mix well. Cook over medium heat, bringing it to a boil. Remove from heat once it boils. When cool, add vanilla (otherwise much of the flavor boils away).

Cost Analysis (30 oz.):
    Homemade = $1.25
    Store-bought = $2.99

My Chewy Granola Bars

    3 C. any granola
    ½ C. honey
    ¹/₃ C. chopped peanuts, other nuts, or chocolate chips
    2 eggs

Combine well and press into a greased 8" x 8" baking pan. Bake at 350° for 20 minutes. Slice into bars after it cools.

Cost Analysis (12 bars):
    Homemade = $2.50
    Store-bought = $4.58

Soft Pretzels

    3½ C. flour
    2 T. sugar
    1 tsp. salt
    2 pkgs. (¼ oz. each) or 4½ tsp. dry yeast
    1 C. water
    1 T. shortening
    1 egg yolk
    1 T. water
    Coarse salt

Mix 1 cup of the flour with the sugar, salt, and dry yeast. In a separate container, heat water and shortening to 120°. Slowly add to the flour mixture. Beat well for 2 minutes. Add ½ cup more flour and beat again for 2 minutes. Stir in the rest of the flour. Knead for 5 minutes. Set in a greased bowl and let rise in a warm place for 40 minutes (or until it doubles in size). Punch down.

Divide the dough into 12 pieces and roll each one into a long rope (18 to 20 inches). Shape into pretzels or other shapes. Place on a greased cookie sheet, and let rest for 5 minutes. Mix egg yolk and 1 T. water. Brush on the pretzels, and sprinkle with the salt. Bake at 375° for 15 minutes.

Cost Analysis (12 soft pretzels):
    Homemade = $1.29
    Store-bought frozen = $3.99

Oatmeal Bread

This is my favorite bread recipe.

    2 pkgs. (¼ oz. each) or 4½ tsp. dry yeast
    1¼ C. warm water
    1¼ C. warm milk
    ½ C. brown sugar
    ½ C. honey
    2 T. vegetable oil
    2 C. quick-cooking oats
    6 C. bread flour
    2 tsp. salt

Dissolve yeast in water and add milk. Add sugar and honey and stir. Add the rest of the ingredients. Mix well. Knead for 5 minutes, then let rise to double in size. Punch down, then knead again. Let rise once more to double in size. Shape into two loaves and let rise to double again. Bake at 350° for 20 minutes.

Cost Analysis (2 loaves):
    Homemade = $3.75
    Store-bought, frozen = $5.38

Tortilla Roll-Ups

This is my favorite hors d'oeuvre recipe.

    1 pkg. 8-inch flour tortillas
    2 pkgs. salmon-flavored cream cheese spread
    1 small can diced black olives
    ½ red onion, diced finely

Spread salmon-flavored cream cheese onto a tortilla. Sprinkle with olives and red onions. Roll up the tortilla as tightly as you can. Slice sections (use a serrated knife for best results) about ½-inch thick. Lay them flat on a platter. They should look like pinwheels. For extra flavor (and cost), add crumbled smoked salmon and capers to the cream cheese.

Cost Analysis (3 dozen):
    Homemade = $7.00
    Store-bought = $14.99

DESSERTS

Funnel Cakes

    2 beaten eggs
    1½ C. milk
    2 C. sifted flour
    1 tsp. baking powder
    ½ tsp. salt
    2 C. cooking oil
    Powdered sugar

Combine eggs and milk. Sift flour, baking powder, and salt

together. Add to egg mixture and beat until smooth. If it is too thick, add milk. If too thin, add flour. Heat oil to 360°. Pour ½ cup of the batter into a funnel and drizzle into the oil, forming a circle with drizzles in the center. Fry until golden brown. Flip, and fry the other side. Drain on paper towel and dust with powdered sugar.

Cost Analysis (makes 6 to 8):
    Homemade = $1.25
    Store-bought = $4.99

Low-Fat Brownies

    ½ C. flour, sifted
    ½ C. unsweetened cocoa powder
    ¼ tsp. salt
    2 large eggs
    1 C. granulated sugar
    ½ C. + 1 T. unsweetened applesauce
    1 T. vanilla

Grease and flour an 8" x 8" square baking pan and set aside. Combine flour, cocoa, and salt. Mix well. In a separate bowl, whisk together eggs, sugar, applesauce, and vanilla. Stir in flour mixture until just blended. Do not overmix. Pour batter into prepared pan. Bake 25 minutes at 325° or until a toothpick inserted in center comes out clean. Cool at least 15 minutes before cutting.

Cost Analysis (1 dozen):
    Homemade = $1.09
    Store-bought = $2.99

SPICES, MIXES, AND SAUCES

Many mixes are simple combinations of spices you probably have in your cupboard. For example, herb mixes for spaghetti sauce seem to be popular. They cost about two dollars per bag. You can make them with a few ingredients and it will cost you an average of forty cents for the same amount.

There are also bulk spice mixes you can buy at warehouse clubs. These are a bargain (as cheap as homemade) if you use the spice often. Most spices last one year on the shelf. Here are some of my favorite mixtures that we use regularly.

Spaghetti Herb Mix

½ C. garlic powder
½ C. onion powder
½ C. dried oregano
3 T. dried basil
3 T. dried thyme
3 T. salt
2 T. sugar

Mix well and store in airtight container. Makes 10 servings or uses. To use, blend 16 oz. diced tomatoes with ¼ cup of the mix.

Taco Spice Mix

¼ C. red pepper flakes or chili powder
¼ C. ground cumin
¼ C. oregano
2 T. cayenne pepper
¼ C. garlic powder
¼ C. onion powder
3 T. salt

Makes 12 servings or uses. To use, add 2 tablespoons to one pound of ground meat. Mix well and then cook. For dips, add 2 tablespoons to 1 cup sour cream or yogurt.

"Ranch" Salad Dressing

   3 garlic cloves, minced
   ¾ C. mayonnaise
   ½ C. buttermilk (or ½ C. milk + ½ tsp. vinegar)
   1 tsp. dried parsley flakes
   1 tsp. onion powder
   ½ tsp. salt
   ½ tsp. pepper

Combine ingredients and blend well until smooth. Chill for at least 30 minutes. Tastes best if chilled overnight before serving.

Cost Analysis (16 oz.):
   Homemade = $1.25
   Store-bought = $3.99

The Best Bleu Cheese Dressing

   1 C. sour cream
   1 tsp. dry mustard
   1 T. black pepper
   1 T. vinegar
   ½ C. milk
   ½ tsp. salt
   ½ tsp. garlic powder
   1 tsp. Worcestershire sauce
   1¹/₃ C. mayonnaise
   4 oz. bleu cheese

Blend all ingredients (except bleu cheese) well. Add cheese in very small pieces and stir well. For maximum flavor, chill for 24 hours before using.

Low-fat alternative: Replace sour cream with plain yogurt.

Cost Analysis (26 oz.):
    Homemade = $3.99
    Store-bought = $8.00

Garlic Croutons

    2 T. butter
    ¼ C. olive oil
    2 large garlic cloves, pressed
    4 bread slices, cut into ¾-inch cubes

Melt the butter and olive oil in saucepan along with the garlic. Place bread cubes in a large mixing bowl. Add butter mixture and mix well. Place on baking sheet and bake at 350° until bread is brown and crisp (20 minutes).

Cost Analysis (24 oz.):
    Homemade = 99¢
    Store-bought = $3.29

Steak Sauce

    1 C. ketchup
    1 garlic clove, minced
    ⅓ C. chopped onion
    ¼ C. each lemon juice, water, Worcestershire sauce, and
        vinegar
    2 T. soy sauce
    2 T. packed dark brown sugar
    1 T. prepared mustard

Combine all ingredients in a saucepan and bring to a boil. Reduce to a simmer and cook for 30 minutes. Refrigerate any leftovers.

Cost Analysis (12 oz.):
Homemade = $1.99
Store-bought = $3.99

MAIN DISHES

Many people have asked what my family eats for dinner. Most assume we live on casseroles and noodles, but we enjoy a variety of foods and flavors. I have found ways to make great meals for less. Here are a few of our favorites.

Pizza

Few of us make our own pizza anymore. Making one from scratch is easy and can cost significantly less than buying one. Here is my favorite recipe:

Dough
1 C. warm water
1 pkg. or 2¼ tsp. dry yeast
1 tsp. sugar
3 C. white (or wheat) flour
2 T. oil (preferably olive)
1 tsp. salt

In a bowl, mix the yeast, sugar, and water, stirring to dissolve the yeast. Let it rest 5 minutes. Add the other ingredients. Knead the dough on a floured board, adding more flour until it's not sticky. Place in a bowl and cover, letting it rise from five minutes to two hours, depending on the texture you would like. The longer you let it rise, the more bread-like the dough will become. Punch down the dough and shape into a large pizza crust.

Dough variations: Mix herbs into the dough. Add 1 T. oregano or dill and 1 tsp. garlic powder.

Topping
Top with any of these combinations and bake at 450° for 15 minutes:

- For a vegetarian pizza, top with tomatoes, marinated artichoke hearts, olives, onions, and bell peppers.
- Brush the dough with olive oil, then sprinkle with basil and oregano.
- Sprinkle with diced chicken, herbs, and a bit of mozzarella cheese.
- Spread pesto over the crust, then layer a thinly sliced zucchini and a few tomatoes. Sprinkle with basil, salt, and pepper.
- Use Monterey jack cheese if mozzarella is not available or price prohibitive.

Cost of dish (serves 4): 99¢ (per crust)

Leftover-Bread Dinner

    3 C. dried bread (broken into cubes)
    4 eggs
    1 can (32 oz.) spinach
    ½ C. shredded cheese (any kind)
    1 tsp. sage
    1 tsp. thyme
    1 tsp. garlic powder
    ½ onion, diced
    1 tsp. salt

Let the bread dry by leaving it out overnight loosely covered with a dish towel. Break it up into a large mixing bowl. Add the rest of the ingredients. Mix well. Put into a greased loaf pan. Bake at 350° for 1 hour. Slice to serve.

Cost of dish (serves 4): $1.99

Poor Man's Steak

> 1 lb. ground beef or turkey
> ½ C. crushed saltine crackers
> ½ C. water
> 2 tsp. salt
> 1 tsp. pepper

Combine all of the ingredients in a bowl and mix well. Pat into thin patties and fry in an ungreased frying pan. Serve as they are, or add a sauce for variety.

Cost of dish (serves 4): $2.25

Potpie

> 1 C. chicken broth
> 1 onion, diced
> 1 potato, peeled and cubed
> 2 carrots, peeled and cubed
> 3 ribs of celery, cubed
> 1 C. leftover cooked chicken, cubed
> 2 T. roux (1 T. butter + 1 T. flour, melted together)
> 1 tsp. sage
> 1 tsp. oregano
> ½ tsp. paprika
> ½ tsp. pepper

Combine all of the ingredients in a pan and stir over low heat until it begins to thicken. Put in a baking dish and spoon the crust (recipe below) on top. Bake at 375° for 45 minutes.

Quick Spooned-On Crust

>1 C. flour
>1½ tsp. baking powder
>½ tsp. salt
>1 C. milk
>1 tsp. vinegar
>½ T. melted butter
>½ tsp. pepper

Combine ingredients and spoon over chicken.

Cost of dish (serves 4): $2.99

Messy Chicken

>1 lb. chicken (about 4 legs with thighs)
>Salt
>2 T. oil
>1 onion, finely chopped
>2 cloves garlic, pressed
>1 tsp. ground cinnamon
>½ tsp. ground cloves
>2 T. brown sugar
>3 small yams or sweet potatoes (1 lb. total), peeled, cubed
>1 tart green apple, peeled, cored, and diced
>1 can (8 oz.) tomato sauce
>½ C. chicken broth
>2 T. apple cider vinegar

Sprinkle chicken lightly on all sides with salt. In a deep frying pan, brown chicken in the oil. Remove chicken and set aside. To the drippings in the pan add onion. Cook until golden. Add garlic, cinnamon, cloves, and brown sugar. Add the chicken, yams, apple, tomato sauce, and chicken broth. Simmer for 45 minutes. Remove chicken, yams, and apple to a serving dish. Stir vinegar into sauce. Heat and stir until sauce is thickened. Pour over chicken. Serve over rice.

Cost of dish (serves 6): $3.75

Fast-Food French Fries

My kids enjoy the taste of McDonald's fries, but I can't drop in a few times a week like we used to. So I learned how to make my fries taste like theirs.

> 2 C. warm water
> 1/3 C. sugar
> 2 large potatoes, cut in strips
> Oil
> Salt

Dissolve sugar in warm water. Place sliced potatoes in the water and let set for 15 to 30 minutes. Heat oil in a deep pan (enough to cover potatoes) to 350°. Dry off all visible water from potatoes and place in oil. Cook for one minute, then remove. This cooks the insides. Let oil return to 350°. Place potatoes back into the oil and cook until golden brown. Remove, drain, and salt to taste.

Cost of dish (serves 2 to 4): 50¢

Fajitas

> ½ lb. chicken breast (or beef strips), sliced
> ½ onion, sliced
> 1 bell pepper, sliced
> 3 cloves garlic, diced or mashed

2 T. oil
2 limes (or lemons), squeeze for juice
1 tsp. chili powder
¼ tsp. ground cumin
½ tsp. salt
½ tsp. pepper
6 large flour tortillas

Toss meat and other ingredients (except tortillas) together and marinate for at least ½ hour (the longer the better). To cook, layer the chicken or beef and vegetables on a broiler pan and place in broiler for a few minutes, or until chicken is done. Discard juices. The meat can also be grilled over the barbecue or pan-fried. If pan-frying, add all of the vegetables and juices to the pan with the meat.

Serve on flour tortillas and roll up like a burrito. For a fancier meal, garnish with guacamole, salsa, sour cream, lettuce, and/or grated cheese.

Cost of meal (serves 4): $4.60

Indian Curry

5 T. butter
½ C. minced onion
6 T. flour
4½ tsp. curry powder
1¼ tsp. salt
1½ tsp. sugar
¼ tsp. ginger
1 C. liquid chicken bouillon
2 C. milk
2 C. meat (can be leftover pieces of chicken, beef, or fish)
1 C. diced apple
1 tsp. lemon juice

Melt butter. Add onion and cook until golden. Add the next five ingredients and stir into a paste. Add bouillon and milk. Cook, stirring until thickened. Add meat, apple, and lemon juice before serving. Serve over brown rice.

Good condiments for curry (if available) are chutney, raisins, chopped peanuts, coconut, diced dried pineapple, diced hard-boiled eggs, and diced pickles (sweet).

Cost of meal (serves 4): $4.00

Chinese Pineapple Chicken

1 lb. chicken breast, diced
1 tsp. cornstarch
pepper
1 garlic clove, crushed
3 tsp. soy sauce
Oil
1 (8 oz.) can pineapple chunks
2 T. water
1 T. cornstarch

Mix chicken with 1 tsp. cornstarch, pepper, garlic, and 1 tsp. soy sauce. Fry chicken in a little oil until underdone. Add pineapple (save the juice for later). Simmer 3 minutes. Set aside. Mix 2 tsp. soy sauce, water, leftover pineapple juice, and 1 T. cornstarch. Add sauce to chicken in pan and cook until thick. Serve on rice.

Cost of dish (serves 4): $4.00

Sandy's Cheese Chile Relleno Puff

2 (4 oz.) cans whole green chilies
8 oz. Monterey jack cheese, shredded
6 eggs

¾ C. milk
1 T. flour
1 tsp. baking powder
½ tsp. garlic salt

Grease a small baking pan. Lay down the chilies and cover with 4 oz. jack cheese. Combine the rest of the ingredients and pour over chilies. Top with rest of cheese. Bake at 350° for 30 minutes or until firm.

Cost of dish (serves 4): $3.75

Leftover Chicken Italian Meal

1 (8 oz.) bag of pasta (bow-tie, macaroni, egg noodles)
1 T. oil (preferably olive)
1 garlic clove, crushed
1 tsp. oregano
1 tsp. thyme
1 lb. leftover cooked chicken, cubed
1 (15 oz.) can stewed tomatoes

Boil pasta until done. Drain. In a skillet, heat oil, garlic, and herbs. Toss in chicken and tomatoes. Heat thoroughly. Toss with pasta. For variation, add frozen corn or diced potatoes to sauce.

Cost of dish (serves 4): $3.79

MEATLESS DISHES

Thai Noodle Meal

8 oz. pasta, any kind
1 C. diced vegetables (use leftovers—carrots, celery, peppers, broccoli)
½ C. chunky peanut butter

3 T. soy sauce
1 T. vinegar (wine, cider, or rice)
½ tsp. hot pepper flakes (or Tabasco sauce, or any hot seasoning mix)
½ C. water

Microwave the vegetables until just tender. Cook pasta and drain. Set aside. Mix the rest of the ingredients in a saucepan. Heat and stir until well mixed and warmed through. Toss with pasta.

Cost of dish (serves 4): $2.79

Anne's Squash Casserole

6 to 8 small zucchini, thinly sliced
2 eggs
1 pkg. saltines, crushed
Salt and pepper to taste
¼ C. grated cheddar cheese

Cook squash and drain. Mash with a fork. Stir in the eggs and salt and pepper. Add enough saltines to absorb liquid. Bake at 325° for 45 minutes. Top with grated cheese.

Note: For a nondairy diet, replace the eggs and cheese with ¾ cup mashed tofu.

Cost of dish (serves 4): $3.99

Vegetarian Chili

1 T. oil
2 cloves garlic, minced
2 onions, chopped
2 (16 oz.) cans stewed tomatoes
2 (16 oz.) cans kidney beans or 2 C. prepared beans
2 green peppers, chopped (optional)

1 (6 oz.) can tomato paste
3 to 4 T. chili powder (depending on how hot you want it)
1 T. cumin seeds or 1 tsp. ground cumin
1 tsp. dried oregano
1 tsp. salt
½ tsp. pepper

Combine oil, garlic, and onions in large pan. Heat until tender. Stir in the rest of the ingredients and simmer for 30 minutes.

Cost of dish (serves 6 to 8): $5.75

My Favorite Vegetable Pancakes

3 C. vegetables, grated or finely chopped (Use what you have or what's in season. For a nice flavor, use mushrooms, zucchini, and leek)
1 C. grated potato
½ onion, grated or diced
4 eggs
Salt and pepper to taste
½ to 1 C. bread crumbs (substitute saltines or flour)
½ C. grated cheese (cheddar adds best flavor, but any will do)

After grating the vegetables, let sit for 15 to 30 minutes. Drain the grated vegetables of all visible water. Add eggs and seasoning; then add bread crumbs until a dough forms. Add cheese and mix well. Form patties and fry in ungreased nonstick pan. You can use a regular pan, but it may require a bit of oil to reduce sticking.

For added zest, drizzle your favorite sauce over the pancakes (salsa, hollandaise, Dijon, tomato basil, etc.).

Cost of dish (serves 4 to 6): $3.50

Easy Microwave Lasagna

    8 lasagna noodles, uncooked
    4 C. (or 32 oz. can) spaghetti sauce
    2 T. wine vinegar
    1 (16 oz.) can spinach + liquid
    16 oz. ricotta or cottage cheese
    1 egg, beaten
    1 tsp. pepper
    1 tsp. oregano
    1 tsp. granulated or dehydrated garlic
    1 C. grated mozzarella cheese

In one bowl, combine spaghetti sauce, vinegar, and spinach and its liquid. In another bowl, combine ricotta, egg, and spices. In two 8" x 8" glass pans, spread ½ cup sauce on the bottom of each pan. Then take 2 uncooked noodles and break to fit across bottom of each pan. Spread ½ cup of egg mixture over noodles. Sprinkle a little cheese over the egg mixture. Cover with ½ cup spaghetti sauce. Repeat layers in the same order, ending with sauce on top. Cover with plastic wrap.

Cook one pan 30 minutes on 50% power in the microwave. When done, let sit covered (for added flavor) while the other cooks.

Note: For a nondairy diet, replace the ricotta cheese and egg with 2¹/₃ cups (18 oz.) mashed tofu, and omit mozzarella cheese or use tofu cheese.

Cost of dish (serves 4): $6.00

Huevos Rancheros

    1 T. vegetable oil
    1 medium onion, diced
    1 clove garlic, minced
    1 can (15 oz.) stewed tomatoes

2 T. chili powder
1 T. oregano
6 eggs
½ C. grated cheddar or Monterey jack cheese

Heat oil in a large skillet and sauté onions and garlic until tender. Add tomatoes and spices. Stir to combine. Add eggs into the sauce, leaving a bit of space between them. Do not break the yolks. Cover pan and simmer, so eggs will poach. When eggs are done, scatter cheese over the eggs and wait until it melts. Serve on rice.

Cost of dish (serves 4): $3.50

Special Beans and Rice

Rice
Prepare rice for four people. Add ½ cup salsa and stir before serving.

Beans
　　1 T. oil
　　1 (32 oz.) can of pinto beans, drained, or 4 C. prepared beans
　　2 oz. Monterey jack cheese (grated)
　　1 T. vinegar (cider)
　　1 T. cayenne pepper
　　3 green onions, diced

Put oil in a frying pan. Pour in beans. Mash beans with a fork. Add cheese. Heat, stirring constantly. When smooth, add vinegar and cayenne; stir and remove from heat. Garnish with green onions.

For a truly authentic meal, prepare a salad using salsa as the dressing.

Cost of dish (serves 4): $2.50

Terry's Lentil Rice Casserole

3 C. water or vegetable broth
¾ C. lentils, uncooked
½ C. brown rice, uncooked
1 onion, chopped
1 T. dry basil
1 T. oregano
1 tsp. thyme
1 tsp. garlic powder (or 2 crushed garlic cloves)
1 T. vegetable seasoning spice
1 T. salt
½ C. grated cheese, tofu cheese, or yogurt (optional)

Combine all ingredients except cheese in a casserole dish. Cover dish with foil. Bake at 300° for 2½ hours. Remove from heat and top with cheese or yogurt before serving.

Cost of dish (serves 4): $1.75

Bean Sandwich Spread

1 (15 oz.) can beans (garbanzo, black, or pinto), drained and rinsed, or 2 C. prepared beans
2 T. yogurt or tofu
½ tsp. chili powder
2 T. onion, chopped
1 T. lemon juice (if using black beans, lime juice is better)
1 garlic clove, crushed

Place all ingredients in a blender and mix to desired consistency (or mash by hand in a bowl). Spread on pita pockets or whole-wheat bread.

Cost of spread: $2.00

CHAPTER 16

Be Wary of Warehouse Clubs

Warehouse clubs are large, plain, unattractive buildings filled with things we think we need. I know people who do 90 percent of their shopping at warehouse clubs, believing they're being thrifty. Unfortunately, warehouse clubs need to be used as carefully as grocery stores. Regardless of what you've heard, they don't have the lowest prices on everything.

These stores are actually private clubs. You pay an annual membership fee for the privilege of shopping there. Almost anyone can join through their credit union, professional club, or employer, or by having a business license. Membership fees are fairly expensive—anywhere from thirty-five to a hundred dollars per year. These clubs have sprung up across the nation, with Costco and Sam's Club owning most of the stores.

Some frugal experts have claimed that these stores only make a profit by charging membership fees. I don't believe this is true. The membership fees help them but are not the only source of income. From what I have read, seen for myself by shopping around, and learned by talking to various employees of these stores, I believe these stores make their profits four ways: membership fees, low overhead (no-frills buildings and minimal staff), high-volume sales of special deals, and high markup on certain items.

Many of the products they sell are inexpensive. But even their prices can often be beat by other retail stores. Sometimes they make a small amount of profit on each item but sell hundreds of thousands of them (at all stores combined), which adds up to a healthy profit. Have you noticed that they often carry only one brand or type of an item? This is not because it's the best one available on the market. They obtain a good deal on a particular product and want to move it as quickly as possible. If they sold any other brand or model of that item, it would compete for sales with that item and they would have extra inventory to carry, and that represents lost profit. This is true of most of their products: there is only one brand of non-chlorine bleach, one brand of bandage, one brand of vacuum cleaner, one phone/fax machine, etc. This is true of their grocery items as well. There are only a few brands available of each food type.

After comparing prices of many like items at our local warehouse clubs with local grocery store prices, I have shortened the list of what I buy at warehouse clubs to only ten or fifteen items. This list changes as they change their prices.

Many of the warehouse club bulk packages are the same price as individually packaged products on sale at grocery stores. This is true of some cereal, diapers, bread, tuna, potato chips, milk, plastic bags, frozen foods, fresh meats, and paper products. (When comparing paper products, don't forget to take the thickness into consideration—one- or two-ply—as well as the number of sheets per roll.) Watch your local stores' bulk section. Many carry a section of bulk-packaged items just like a warehouse club. Many times the local store will charge the same or less than the warehouse club.

Knowing your prices is crucial. The packages are larger than we are used to, and it's harder to determine if it's a good deal. Some things are cheaper, but many things are actually more expensive than at regular grocery stores. Taking your price list along helps. Many people fall into the trap of thinking everything is less at a warehouse club than at a regular grocery store, so they buy whatever they need or want. This can be financially deadly. For example, one warehouse club sells their own brand of paper products at 2.5 times higher (that's 250 percent) than its equivalent at local stores. I also think the quality of these paper products is inferior to items I buy elsewhere for less. These higher prices are scattered throughout the store. A good example of this is name-brand over-the-counter drugs. On my last visit I compared the price of Bayer aspirin and found that the unit price of the jumbo size I would have to buy at the warehouse club cost more than at the local grocery store. You need a calculator and your price list for safe maneuvering.

Want warehouse club prices without the membership fees? Shop online at Web sites that offer case pricing and deliver to you. Check out *www .buythecase.net.*

When we compare items, we must remember that store-brand equivalents sell at a much lower price. Warehouse clubs mainly sell well-advertised name brands. This alone makes their prices higher on many items. A warehouse club will usually be cheaper if you only compare the name brands to their prices at a grocery store. But we must not forget the great alternatives found in generic and store brands.

Occasionally a warehouse club will sell their own brand (beyond the paper products mentioned above). Many of these brands are equally as good as the name-brand equivalent. Some off brands are even the same item. Many companies buy items from the name-brand corporations and sell them under their own label. The store has eliminated the middleman and can sell for less than any competitor and still make a good profit. The warehouse clubs know this and are beginning to add more of their own brands. The quality of most store-brand items is improving greatly. They know you won't settle for less, so they continually improve the flavors, textures, and durability of their goods.

Warehouse clubs should be a tool just like other resources. They should be used only for those things that cost less. When I stick to this plan, I stay within my budget. But I am as easily tempted as anyone. And warehouse clubs can be very tempting. I tend to overbuy foods when I shop at these stores. I buy more of some items than we normally need, and the food is consumed as quickly as when I buy less—even when we aren't hungry. If it's there, we eat it. I am tempted by the convenience foods that are cheaper than at grocery stores. But I must remind myself that making them at home is even cheaper—and healthier. And I must remind myself of my goal, my reason for making that choice.

I often am asked if joining a warehouse club is worth the cost. I believe the answer is yes. It is a fair question that each person needs to calculate. I don't like that I have to pay to shop at a store, but if I am careful about what I buy, I come out ahead every year. If you watch your prices and buy only those items that are good buys, it is worth it, and you will recoup your membership fee and more. Otherwise, if you buy everything your home needs at this type of store, you could be paying a membership fee in order to spend as much as you would at a regular grocery store.

Another factor to consider before deciding to shop at these types of stores is whether you can handle the temptations. If you are an impulse shopper, you will do better to shop elsewhere. The good deals are not worth it. The overwhelming nature of these stores can cause you to spend more than you would if you had shopped at a regular store.

To help you maneuver through the aisles of these warehouse

stores, I have listed good buys and bad buys. I tried to pick commonly used items. This is by no means a complete list. It will merely help you to start your own research. Remember that each store's prices may vary and prices change weekly in some areas.

GOOD DEALS (A GOOD SALE PRICE) AT A WAREHOUSE CLUB

- Store-brand over-the-counter drugs:
  acetaminophen (1.6¢ per pill)
  aspirin (2.1¢ per pill)
  ibuprofen (1.7¢ per pill)
- Spices and gravy mixes (25¢ to 40¢ per serving)
- Batteries ($1.75 per 4-pack)
- Most peanut butters (8.3¢ per oz.)
- Milk ($3.05 per gal.)
- Lunch meat (19.7¢ per oz.)
- Salad dressing (11¢ per oz.)
- Canned vegetables (varies)
- Jams (5¢ per oz.)
- Flour (27¢ per lb.)
- Chocolate chips (11¢ per oz.)
- Office supplies (varies)
- Pet food (60¢ per lb.)
- Bulk candy (variety bags)

Some convenience items may be good buys at warehouse clubs, but I didn't list these because they are items I don't buy (cheaper to make them).

I also found many items to be comparably priced to grocery

store prices and did not list them, since the point of this list was to say what was a better/good deal at warehouse clubs.

BAD DEALS (CAN FIND ON SALE FOR LESS ELSEWHERE) AT A WAREHOUSE CLUB

- Name-brand over-the-counter drugs:
  Advil (4.2¢ per pill)
  Tylenol (4.2¢ per pill)
- Household cleaning products (varies)
- Vegetable oil (store brand is cheaper)
- Light bulbs ($1.08 per bulb)
- Plastic bags (store brand is cheaper)
- Most paper products:
  toilet paper (51¢ per roll)
  tissues ($1.35 per box of 100)
  paper towels ($1.42/roll)
- Most boxed cereal (16¢ per oz. vs. 10¢ (on sale) at regular store for same)
- Sugar (50¢ per lb.)
- Frozen chicken ($2.66 or higher per lb.)
- Fresh meat (varies)
- Eggs ($2.70 per dozen)
- Frozen concentrated juices ($1.41 per can)
- Bottled juices (varies)
- Candy (varies)
- Laundry detergent (18¢ per load)

To compare these prices with my target prices, revisit the Price Goals chart in chapter 5, "Keep Track of Food Prices."

CHAPTER 17

Stretch the Season

Gardening is the number one hobby in America, and it is also a good way to cut grocery costs. I know friends who have converted one of the yards (back or front) of their home into a large vegetable garden. These friends grow their own produce and don't buy any fruits or vegetables all summer. One friend calculated the cost of each organic tomato she grew at one cent each.

If you don't have a large yard, plant a small garden. Many magazines have special editions on how to use a small space to produce vegetables. A four-by-eight-foot raised garden box can produce an abundant harvest. I use every space, including along the fence, where I grow berry vines. Don't limit yourself to the dirt on the ground. I have also used hanging pots to grow produce. I had a series of pots running around the eaves of my house; I grew strawberries, carrots, cherry tomatoes, and herbs. If you have no yard at all, many cities offer a community plot. There are sometimes two to three lots per city. They give you a large plot of your own, all the water you need, and free mulch for a low annual fee.

For those who want to try a hand at converting their yard into a garden, here are some cost-saving tips.

- Fertilizer is free from horse stables and chicken farms.
- Mulch is free in some cities if they have a recycling program.
- Make your own compost in a small container. There are books at the library on how to do this.
- For bedding borders, collect rocks at a local creek.
- Seeds go on sale in March at most stores. Many avid gardeners, however, recommend ordering seeds from catalogs. They say the quality is better.

Some types of seeds (not "hybrid" seeds) can be successfully harvested and replanted the following year. Be careful on storage—seeds don't like it too hot or too cold.

To decide which vegetable or fruit to grow, look at the amount of yard needed, the yield the item will give you, and the climate. For example, a zucchini plant takes up a very large area, but a tomato vine does not. But both require a hot climate and won't do well in cool areas. There are even hybrid plants that grow several vegetables and fruits together. Some smart farmers have grafted fruit tree limbs of several types to one trunk, allowing a good harvest out of limited space. I have even heard of tomato plants with potato plants grafted onto them so that above ground you get one type of vegetable and below ground you get another.

The main challenge of growing your own produce, or having friends who do, is the sudden surplus of one item. What do you do with thirty pounds of tomatoes all at once? One way to avoid this problem is to plant in shifts. Plant one row one week, another the next week, etc., so they ripen in shifts as well. If you are the recipient of bushels of produce from generous friends, there are ways to stretch the produce to last all year. Remember that our farming ancestors learned this art. That's how they had food all year round. Preserving is done by salting, pickling, canning, freezing, and drying. I recommend these methods if you have an abundance of any food item. You won't need to buy that food again all year.

To preserve my bounty, I make a bunch of meals or snacks from that one food item and then freeze them. For example, I'll make a ton of jam, zucchini bread, and tomato sauce. I then have what I need all year. Following are some tips I selected from my notes. They are mainly for excess zucchini, pumpkin, tomatoes, and fruits. I picked these produce items because they are the most commonly grown in home gardens.

ZUCCHINI

Zucchini can be frozen but will be mushy when thawed. I freeze them in the form I will use them when thawed. I grate them or slice them and store in meal-sized portions. Good uses for zucchini are zucchini pancakes, zucchini bread, zucchini relish, and spaghetti sauce with grated zucchini in it.

TOMATOES

- Select firm, tight-skinned tomatoes with deep color. They should feel heavy. "Light" feeling tomatoes are usually pulpy with little taste.

- If you have unripened tomatoes on the vine, but frost is imminent, pull up the whole vine and hang it upside down in a cool, dark place. They will ripen slowly over a few weeks.

- When cooking with fresh tomatoes, avoid aluminum pans, which can react with the acid in tomatoes to create an unpleasant taste.

- In cooked tomato dishes, a pinch of sugar enhances the flavor.

- Never wash a tomato until just before use. Washing increases the risk of spoilage.

- To peel a tomato, try these two easy ways: First, place the tomato in boiling water for thirty seconds, then place in cold water. The skins will pull right off. Another method adds flavor to the tomato. Place the tomato on the end of a fork and hold it over a gas flame, turning constantly, until the skin blisters. Pull the skin off with a paring knife.

- Freeze any tomatoes not needed. Freeze them whole and when fully ripened (remove stems first). When they thaw, the skin falls right off and the fruit has the texture of a stewed tomato.

- Make and freeze large batches of salsa, spaghetti sauce, or tomato soup.

- Many enjoy picking tomatoes when they are green and frying them, a southern dish. To make fried green tomatoes, dip green tomato slices in flour or cornmeal. Fry in oil until golden. For the best flavor, fry in bacon drippings.

PUMPKIN

To cook a pumpkin, cut it in half and scrape out the seeds. Place the two halves (open side down) on a cookie sheet and bake in a slow oven (300°) until tender (20 to 40 minutes). Scrape out the pumpkin and discard the shells. Use the cooked pumpkin the same way as you would canned pumpkin. This can be used to make pumpkin bread, pumpkin pancakes, pumpkin pie, pumpkin cheesecake, and pumpkin tomato soup. Pumpkin seeds are a favorite in our house. We toss oil and salt on them and bake until golden brown.

FRUITS

Lemons—When I get bags of lemons from friends, I juice them all and freeze the juice in ice-cube trays. Then I pop the cubes into plastic bags and keep them year round for whenever I need lemon juice for cooking or lemonade. One cube is the juice of about half a lemon.

Apples—When my mom's apple tree is in season, we eat the best of them and store the rest by making applesauce (simply boil them down and mash with a fork), cobbler, or apple butter, or I freeze slices in plastic bags for pies or I dry them (thinly slice and lay on baking sheet; bake overnight at 200°).

Berries—Growing your own berries is the best way to enjoy these lovely fruits. When a berry is vine-ripened, it is much sweeter than any store-bought version. If you cannot grow your own, visit a local farm that allows you to pick your own fruit. The raspberries and strawberries we picked were priced 75 percent less than the store's price. We made jam and cobblers that lasted for months. Making jam is the best way to use up extra fruits before they spoil. Frozen fruit pops, fruit leather, and fruit juice are also great uses for extra fruit.

Cranberries—After Thanksgiving, fresh cranberries go on sale. Buy several bags of these to make into juice or jelly. They can be frozen for up to one year.

Homemade cranberry sauce is preferred at our house over the canned variety. Make a bunch and freeze the extra. Who says cranberry sauce can be used only at Thanksgiving? Aside from enjoying it with foods as a condiment, it is a good recipe base. My favorite meatball recipe combines 2 pounds of meatballs with 2 cups of cranberry sauce and ½ cup of chili sauce.

Resources

The Complete Idiot's Guide to Gardening, Jane Connor and Emma Sweeney (Alpha Books, 1996).

The Frugal Gardener: How to Have More Garden for Less Money, Catriona Tudor Erler (Rodale Press, 2001).

Low-Cost Gardening, Ian Walls (Ward Lock, 1992).

Rodale Complete Garden Problem-Solver: Instant Answers to the Most Common Gardening Questions, Cheryl Long (Rodale Press, 1998).

Rodale Organic Gardening Solutions: Over 500 Answers to Real Life Questions From Backyard Gardeners, Cheryl Long (Rodale Press, 2000).

Stocking Up: How to Preserve the Foods You Grow, Naturally, Carol Stoner (Rodale Press, 1973).

CHAPTER 18

Marketing Tricks That You Need to Know

A good deal is a good deal only when it's a good deal. Confusing? It sure is. If we believe the marketing agencies, everything is a good deal. And unless you are a savvy consumer, you will believe them and buy what they want you to buy. It's getting tougher and tougher to navigate what is truly a good deal and what is hype. Market researchers spend hundreds of thousands of dollars learning how to make people buy things that they weren't going to buy in the first place. So we need to be working to not fall for their tricks. Hopefully, this will help you learn some tricks of the trade and make you more aware of what to look for.

One research finding revealed that how happy you were with the purchase at the time, compared to your options available, determines how good of a deal you think you obtained. If we are presented with inferior products, we will pick the best of the inferior products and say we got the best one. But we don't think past the options in front of us to better products within that category. This is how things work in the warehouse clubs. I mentioned in an earlier chapter that they sell only one or two of some product mainly because they need to move the inventory they have bought. But it also helps to make the consumers feel that they got a good deal if they have nothing to compare it to at the time.

It pays to know your products before you buy so that you can recognize a true good deal.

When is a sale a sale?

I mentioned earlier that often a store will say something is on sale, but the price really is not a sale price. Researchers have been documenting this fact for years. If a store says it's a sale, people flock in and buy it—even if it's not a good price. Furniture stores are notorious for this trick. They often have a 50-percent-off sign featured. But the savvy consumer would know that furniture is usually marked up by over that amount, making 50 percent off no better than full retail at many stores. Knowing your prices pays off.

Know when you are being manipulated

There are many ways marketing companies and salespeople get you to buy things that you weren't planning on buying in the first place. Some of these tricks are more obvious, such as putting impulse items near the registers, putting toys on the bottom shelf of the cereal aisle at children's eye level, and placing the most expensive items at eye level but the cheaper ones higher and lower on the shelves. Others might be less obvious, like directing you to begin shopping at a certain end of the store. This way all items on your right will be of a higher price. (We tend to look more to our right.) And have you noticed that essentials like bread and milk are at the back of the stores so you have to walk past other items to get there? The more you know what is being tried on you, the better you will be at avoiding these pitfalls to the budget.

The most common way marketers manipulate you is by

convincing you that you are getting a great deal. As I mentioned earlier, whether it is a good deal or not is irrelevant. If they can convince you it is, they win. One way they try to convince you is to not offer much competition for that item, so the item they want to sell you appears to be the best deal. As I mentioned before, warehouse clubs often offer only one or two of an item (vacuums, pans, dishes, etc.). It is hard to compare them to anything when you are in the store, so you assume that you are being presented with a great deal. Another trick salesmen use is to offer you an item at an obviously high price (like a computer cable for $100). Once you complain, they show you the $50 version, which you gladly take, thinking you have just saved $50. If you had done the research, you would have found the $10 cable at another store. But the store that overcharged you intentionally does not carry the $10 version so they can accurately claim that the $50 version is all they have.

Another way salespeople sell you something that you never intended to buy is when they ask you which of the items you are looking at appeals to you the most. This question implies that you will purchase one of them. The non-savvy buyer will be persuaded to buy one when they were just looking.

And what about our noses? We have all smelled the baking bread in the stores at 4:00 p.m., which intensifies our already hungry stomach. But it goes further than that. Our noses tend to guide us in many ways. Research done by the *Journal of Consumer Research* concludes that the smell trigger causes us to opt for immediate pleasure—of any type. The research concluded that "the stimulus could induce a general motivational state . . . which focuses one's attention on the immediate environment. [This state] propels a consumer to choose smaller-sooner options in unrelated domains" (February 2008, Vol. 34, No. 5; pp 649–656). More plainly put, when a research group was exposed to a hidden candle that smelled like chocolate chip cookies, they impulsively bought sweaters they neither planned on buying nor had the budget to do so. Real estate agents and home staging companies also recommend that homes smell like chocolate chip cookies prior to being shown for sale.

One of the sneakier tricks is to recommend that you use a larger amount or more of something so that you buy it more frequently. Toothpaste commercials are a great example, showing you an inch-long strip of toothpaste on the toothbrush when a pea-sized amount is all that is needed. For over 150 years, Arm & Hammer has recommended that a box of their baking soda be put in America's refrigerators to combat odor, and that the box be changed every three months. These boxes have always contained 100 percent pure baking soda. The ingredient in the boxes has not changed. But now Arm & Hammer recommends that you change the box every month. When asked, they give no direct answer as to why the recommendation has changed. Folgers has reduced the size of their coffee cans by four ounces but is claiming that the smaller can makes twenty cups *more* than the previous can did. The brewing instructions did not change, so how are they doing the math?

Did our food go through a shrink ray?

Some consumers are lulled into a false sense of consumer safety, assured that their overall grocery bill hasn't increased too much. Yet with some closer examination, they would see that the bill might have remained the same, but what they took home was much less than it used to be. Reducing the size and contents of a package while leaving the package price the same is the latest way manufacturers are raising prices without raising attention. Kraft salad dressing bottles are 19 percent smaller than before but cost the same. Coca-Cola bottles are 34 percent smaller now, but there was no reduction in price. These changes have saved the manufacturers millions of dollars, but little of that savings is being passed on to the consumer.

As I have mentioned earlier, any prepackaged item is going to cost you more than making it yourself. One of the reasons is that the package sometimes costs significantly more than the contents of the package. So altering the package is where the savings lies for these companies. Lessening the amount of plastic a bottle uses will save the company more than charging a few cents more for the contents. Sadly, they are reducing both the package size and the contents in the package.

Other examples of the shrinking packaging are:

- Hellmann's mayonnaise went from 32 ounces to 30 ounces
- Country Crock spread went from 3 pounds to 2 pounds 13 ounces
- Costco's frozen chicken breast went from 3-breast pouches to 2-breast pouches
- Quilted Northern toilet tissue went from 440 sheets per roll to 352
- Nature Valley chewy granola bars went from 35 bars per box to 30
- Hefty kitchen trash bags went from 40 bags per box to 34
- Subway sandwiches are now getting one less slice of meat for every 6 inches of sandwich
- Tropicana orange juice went from 96-ounce jugs to 89-ounce jugs
- Pampers diapers went from 80 diapers per package to 72
- Lucerne yogurts went from 8 ounces per container to 6 ounces

These changes create a significant increase in the unit price of the items . . . anywhere from a 17 percent to 25 percent increase. Often these items have a huge sale sign hanging on them offering some discount, but the discount doesn't outweigh the increase in unit price. It's like a maze, and if you aren't careful you'll get lost and just give up.

The change works the other way as well. Manufacturers will increase the content of the package and overly increase the price. Proctor and Gamble did this with their Gillette Mach 3 blade refill pack. They went from 4 per pack to 5 per pack, but increased the unit price of the blades by 21 cents per blade. This is why knowing unit prices is the key to all smart shopping.

CHAPTER 19

Celebrating With a Frugal Flair

When it's time for a special occasion, we tend to throw the budget out the window. We think things like *Oh, it's their birthday* or *But it's Christmas!* I think we try to make ourselves feel better about not being creative at times like these.

Should we be sending the message that love and money are related? I have found that what people really want are your efforts and thoughts toward them. A simple party and homemade gifts mean more than extravagance. I think the same goes for our kids. A room full of toys is overwhelming. A few well-chosen items are better received.

So how do I keep the gift and party madness from putting me in debt for months? First, I plan what we are going to spend. I list all of the people we usually buy gifts and/or cards for (birthdays and holidays) for the entire year, any expected graduation or wedding gifts, baby showers, and the parties we usually throw (birthday, Christmas, Thanksgiving, monthly church potluck, etc.). Then we decide the maximum amount we will spend on each person for each occasion. We then add up the year's total and divide by twelve. This gives us the amount we need to set aside each month in order to achieve those goals. If it's too much for our budget, we scale back on certain events or gifts and stick to it.

Then we apply some creative and fun ideas to make a frugal event special. Following are some ideas I have used for birthdays, holidays, and other special events. I hope they help your household.

HOLIDAYS

If there's one theme I hope I've gotten across in my books, it's that being frugal does not mean we have to do without or look cheap. This is true in every area of our home—holidays included! We can have a beautiful home that fills our guests with warmth during the holidays. Here are some ideas we have used in our home to enjoy the holidays in their grandeur and stay within our budget.

CHRISTMAS

This is my favorite time of year. We celebrate this holiday for a month in our home. I love the look, smells, and sounds of Christmas. The reason for the season—Jesus' birth—makes this a meaningful time of year. You can tell how much I love this holiday by how much more space I dedicate to it compared to the other holidays.

Decorating

To give your home a festive feel, try adding something natural from the season. I fill a basket with pinecones and string some simple white tree lights around and through the basket. Sometimes I spray-paint the cones gold or silver. This basket can be large and set by the front door or fireplace, or it can be small and placed in the center of a table.

Bring evergreen boughs into the house. If you don't have

any evergreens in your yard, cut a lower limb off your Christmas tree and trim it so that it can be laid on the mantel, around staircase banisters, around a lamppost, or over a large framed picture. You can also purchase plastic boughs that are inexpensive and easy to use. Decorate them with small white tree lights or ribbons.

We also string tiny white lights around houseplants or window frames. And don't forget the wreaths! Make them with boughs, or wire together any type of branch (artificial or real) in a circular shape. Hang them inside or outside. The more the merrier!

What to do with all those cards that come in the mail? We turn them into part of the Christmas decorations. Sometimes we put them in a lovely basket (spray-paint an old one with gold or silver paint) with a ribbon tied to the handle. Other times we have strung a ribbon along the hallway or above the fireplace and hung the cards over the ribbon. Some people hang corkboard over a doorway and tack the cards to it. We try to reuse the cards as gift tags the next year: Cut the picture on the card with pinking shears and punch a hole in one corner for the ribbon.

For the table, have the children help make decorative items. They can wrap tiny boxes to place around an evergreen bough. Wrap a cardboard tube from a toilet paper roll with foil or white paper to make a paper angel. Cut some wings from paper and glue them to the back. Have the children draw on faces. The guests will enjoy seeing their artwork. Check out a book on napkin folding from the library. This free activity can make a beautiful table.

I put scented candles in the guest bathroom and kitchen, on the dining table, and wherever else they look inviting. (If there are small children or perfume-allergic people in your home, you may want to avoid this tip.)

Entertaining

The focus should be on the friends and relatives, not the food and gifts. To scale down the cost of entertaining, try to change the type of party you have. Instead of serving dinner, serve dessert or have tea. Or have an hors d'oeuvre party with some inexpensive items. There are many good cookbooks at the library and Web sites that specialize in inexpensive hors d'oeuvre recipes. If you want to serve a dinner, make the main dish and let others bring the side dishes. Or make dishes with less meat in them, or meatless altogether (try a vegetarian lasagna, for example).

Creating Memories

The best part about Christmas for me is the memories my friends and family make together. Traditions that we create with our own hands and then hand down; the ties we make with family over time. There are so many things we can do to make this time of year special. I have pages and pages of ideas and have selected a few of our favorites for your family to try.

The music of this season is so special. I fill the house with Christmas songs all day (if the family will let me!). I go to the library every year and select several CDs (go early; they go fast!). My favorite is Handel's *Messiah*. I love to hear it, but most of all I love why it was written. Did you know that this oratorio is about the prophecies that led up to the Messiah's (Jesus') birth? And that the famous "Hallelujah Chorus" celebrates the fulfilled prophecies? Research the Bible verses the songs are based on. It is great to read those verses as a family before listening to each song and understand what they are singing about.

While you are at the library researching these songs, read about Christmas traditions in other countries. It's fascinating! Also find a book on the story of the candy cane and its inventor.

Crafts are such an important part of Christmas for my children and me. We make ornaments, gingerbread houses, centerpieces, wreaths, and anything else we can think of. Some of our favorites are listed:

- Buy terra-cotta clay, roll it a half-inch thick, and cut ornaments out with cookie cutters. Poke a hole in the top so you can run a ribbon through it. Air-dry overnight. Draw faces and write names of friends with puff paint and give as gifts.

- Make cinnamon dough (1½ cups cinnamon, 1 cup applesauce, ⅓ cup white school glue) and form into ornaments or snowmen for table decorations. Let air-dry two to three days.

- Create a photo ornament of each child every year. Make the frame from funny foam, Popsicle sticks, a decorated lid from frozen juice concentrate, or even construction paper.

- Make your own Christmas cards for special people or the elderly, who will appreciate your personal touch.

- Make a snow globe. We have done it two ways: one with water and one without. With water requires a baby food jar, glitter, and a small toy for the center. Fill the jar with water and some glitter, and glue the toy to the inside of the lid (the lid will become the bottom of the globe). Once the jar is closed, hot-glue around the edges so nothing can be opened or leak. For the waterless type, take a plastic bubble container that comes in gumball or vending machines. Find a tiny toy that fits inside the bubble. Glue the toy to the lid of the bubble. With a toothpick, dot white paint on the inside of the bubble to represent snow. Then glue the lid to the bubble.

- Make your own Advent calendar: Draw twenty-five (one-inch) pictures on a large piece of construction paper (or glue on pictures from old Christmas cards). Take another piece of paper the same size and cut windows where the pictures will be. Glue the corners of the paper together and let the kids open one frame per day.

Crafts aren't the only way to build memories. You could start a family journal that is written in only at Christmastime (keep it with the decorations and bring it out each year). Write what each person wants for Christmas, how tall the children are, what their interests are that year, what they want to be when they grow up, etc.

Start a keepsake box for each child. Every year add an ornament for each of the children. The boxes can be given to them when they have their own tree.

To help the family understand and celebrate the reason for Christmas, celebrate it in a special way. Have an Advent wreath with candles to celebrate the month leading up to Christmas. Make a birthday cake for Jesus using colors and shapes to signify the uniqueness of His birthday: make a star-shaped cake; the icing can be white for purity or gold for royalty, and layers of the cake can be different colors for different symbols.

Watch some classic Christmas movies together. Get some from the library (they're free or inexpensive!). Some of our favorites are *Miracle on 34th Street, A Christmas Carol,* and *Veggie Tales: The Toy That Saved Christmas.*

If getting outside is the best way for your family to bond, try a few of these Christmas activities:

- Have a Christmas caroling party. Invite the neighbors and visit your neighborhood or a nursing home. Offer warm drinks and cookies afterward.

- Visit a living nativity scene in your town.

- Adopt a family that is having a hard time financially. Deliver food, gifts, or decorations to them. To find a family that wants this help, contact your church, Chamber of Commerce, or local charities.

- Celebrate Boxing Day. This holiday began in early England, according to some historians. On the day after Christmas, the churches would open their poor boxes and share the money with the poor. Later, in the Middle Ages, the gentry would wrap gifts they didn't want and give them to their servants. This day became known as St. Stephen's Day, honoring the memory of this saint who was martyred. Use this day to give gifts to those who may not have much. Fill a box with things you aren't using and donate them to a local charity.

- Have a talent show for the family or invite the neighbors. Videotape it and show it every year.

Gifts

Gift giving shouldn't be something we dread or do with obligation. It should flow from our love for others. But sometimes our wallet stops us from showing those feelings as freely as we'd like. That doesn't mean we can't give gifts. Our family has tackled this issue a number of ways. I already shared how we budget how much we want to spend on Christmas gifts and then put some of that money aside every month throughout the year. Another tip we have used is to encourage family members to draw names for gift giving so that the one gift we give can be nicer, and no guilt is felt if we can't get a gift for everyone. Other ideas have been to require that the gift be made by the giver. That could include a craft, a poem, a letter of appreciation, etc. One year I made scrapbooks of each family member's major events in their life. (Use a three-ring binder, acid-free plastic sleeves, acid-free glue, and stickers on acid-free paper.)

I still believe the same principle that applies to children's gifts applies to adult gifts. What people want is thought and effort, not money or expensive gifts. I try to make my gifts for friends and relatives, and I aim to make these gifts throughout the year and keep them on hand. That way I am less busy during the holidays, I am less tempted to buy a last-minute item for someone, and I have gifts on hand for birthdays and other events throughout the year.

Some gift ideas require making the item at the time it is needed, such as baked fruit breads. You can bake these as regular-sized loaves or use mini baking tins and give a variety of breads. Wrap them in colored plastic wrap and tie each with a bow for added appeal.

When a baked or homemade item is inappropriate, I buy something on sale. Shopping in advance of the holidays allows you to watch for sales. I try never to pay full price. Waiting to shop near the holiday may cost more. The item you want may not be on sale then, and you'll be tempted to pick items you wouldn't normally buy.

Here are some of my favorite homemade gifts. I hope they inspire you:

- One of my favorite gifts to make is a teacup candle. I look through thrift stores and garage sales for a decorative teacup-and-saucer set and find two votive candles of a color complementary to the pattern on the cup. I hot-glue the cup to the saucer, then melt the candles (in something I can throw away when done) in a double boiler over the stove (be careful not to spill wax on the stove). When the candles are melted, I remove the wick and hang it in the center of the cup from a pencil that is resting across the edges of the cup. Then pour the melted wax into the teacup and let it harden. This makes a lovely gift and can be accompanied by a bookmark or bookstore gift certificate.

- Make a sachet from a small piece of fabric (four inches by four inches) with a simple ribbon tie. Fill it with any of the following: rose petals, cotton balls with a few drops of vanilla extract drops on it, cinnamon sticks with orange peels and cloves, or lavender flowers.

- Do you have a family recipe that has been handed down for generations? Make it for your friends and wrap the results in a colorful gift container.

- Save seeds from your garden, fold paper into a seed packet, and give with a garden tool attached.

- Make some solid perfumes in pillboxes: melt two parts Vaseline with one part paraffin, and add a few drops of essential oil.

- Make stepping-stones from plaster of Paris with handprints or shells or jewels.

- Make a pincushion jar filled with buttons, and top with a cotton-filled fabric cover on the lid.

- Make herbed vinegar by filling tall attractive jars with distilled vinegar and adding herbs from your garden. Seal the lid with hot wax.

Whatever gift you choose to make can be presented in a decorative fashion and given alone or combined with other gifts in a basket.

Themed Baskets

Another way to show your thoughtfulness and attention to the recipient is to give a basket filled with a variety of items that all revolve around a certain theme. Think of something that your recipient likes to do and get items that support that interest. The basket can even be a part of the theme (a bucket, a bag, a colander, or even a backpack). To help you create a unique, beautiful basket, I have listed a few themes below.

Finding the baskets isn't that hard: I buy them at thrift

shops and garage sales. Sometimes I spray-paint them gold or silver to spruce them up a bit. Then fill the bottom with straw, shredded leftover wrapping paper, confetti paper found at party stores, or a piece of cloth with the edges cut with pinking shears. Recipes for some of the gifts listed here can be found throughout this book.

Themed Gift Baskets

Italian Gift Basket

- Spiral pasta
- Pasta spoon
- Spaghetti sauce
- Italian seasoning mix
- Garlic bulbs
- Fresh tomatoes
- Cheese grater
- Recipe card for a pasta dish
- Instead of a basket, place the items in a large colander

Latte Lover's Basket

- Coffee mug
- Instant beverage mixes
- Chocolate-dipped spoon
- Biscotti

Movie Lover's Basket

- Two microwave popcorn bags
- Chocolate bar
- Sodas
- Movie theater pass or movie rental certificate

- Instead of a basket, place all of these items in a popcorn bowl

Bread Lover's Basket

- Loaf of gourmet bread
- Bread mixes ready for bread machine
- Wooden mixing spoon
- Cutting board

S'mores Lover's Basket

- Graham crackers
- Marshmallows
- Chocolate bars
- A skewer or nice twigs for roasting marshmallows
- Instead of a basket, wrap these items in a scarf

Bath Lover's Basket

- Scented bath salts
- Sea sponge
- Scented candle

Pet Lover's Basket

- Homemade dog treats
- Dog toy
- Dog brush
- Homemade pet bed/blanket

College Student's Basket

- Various snack foods
- Hot cocoa, chai, and other instant hot drink mixes
- Gift card to a fast-food restaurant

- Prepaid phone card
- Gift certificate to gas stations

Car Lover's Basket

- Shop towels
- Goop hand cleaner
- Car-washing soap
- Sponges
- Window-washing solution
- The basket could be a bucket

Child's Busy Basket

- Homemade play dough
- Homemade Gak
- Cookie cutters
- Sidewalk chalk
- Bubbles
- Crayons
- Silly Putty
- Sand bucket as basket

Child's Dress-Up Box

Look at thrift stores for:

- Hats
- Uniforms
- Fancy dresses
- Costumes
- Costume jewelry
- Handbags

- Plastic swords

Teenage Girl's Basket

- Nail polish
- Lip gloss
- Bubble bath
- Scented bath salts
- Key chains
- Chocolate

Hunter/Camper's Basket

- Granola
- Biscuit mix
- Soup mix
- Flavored coffee mix
- Mug or bowl
- Disposable hand and feet warmers

Spice Basket

- Homemade Mexican seasoning mix, spaghetti sauce mix, or Italian seasoning mix in a decorative jar
- Wooden spoon
- The basket could be a mixing bowl

Get-Well Basket

- Jar of homemade chicken noodle soup mix
- Soup bowl
- Good book
- Vitamin C
- Kleenex tissue

I try to stock up at the after-Christmas sales on wrapping paper. These are usually 50 to 75 percent off. I also look for alternative types of paper to use. If you live near a paper factory or stationery manufacturer, they sometimes have ends of large rolls of paper to give away. Wallpaper stores have sheets of samples that make elegant-looking paper. We have made our own paper by buying white butcher paper and stamping, drawing, and hand printing on it. My grandmother used the Sunday comics and raffia—this has a country feel. She also used large pieces of fabric, trimmed the edges with pinking shears, and tied them with ribbon.

THANKSGIVING

Decorating

This time of year it is easy to incorporate the colors and fruits of nature in our decorating. Indian corn, colored leaves, straw, etc., can all be used to make a home more festive. I change the theme of my front door wreath by sticking branches with colored fall leaves in it.

The first area that I focus on is my table centerpiece. This can be an arrangement of Indian corn, leaves, miniature squash, and candles. Or you can be more elaborate and make some crafts to complete the arrangement. Make candle holders from apples (must be made very close to dinnertime). Make placemats from different colored leaves, stamping, and magazine cutouts laminated to construction paper. Make miniature scarecrows from baby or doll clothes: fill them with straw and have them sit on miniature pumpkins.

Have the children make name cards for each guest, complete with hand-drawn decorations. Make a list of the guests' names for them to work from. Then have them make napkin rings from toilet paper tubes: decorate them with paint, foil, stickers, etc.

Making Memories

As with Christmas, celebrating the holiday should be intertwined with understanding the reason for the day. Reading stories of the day's history not only brings us together but also helps us appreciate it more. Read about a day in the life of a Pilgrim or study the different types of Native American lifestyles from the northeast as compared to the Native Americans who live in your region. Use the public library for books on the holiday. Some of my favorites are listed in the resource section at the end of this chapter.

Create a Thanksgiving tablecloth that you can use each year. Start with a light-colored cloth (can be muslin) and cut and hem it to fit your table. Each year have guests write on the cloth with colored fabric pens. They can simply sign their name or write a brief thank-you note. I found my grandmother's tablecloth with this theme, and it is so special to see the names of past family members.

There are many more things we can do on Thanksgiving to learn what the Pilgrims did. Here are some of my favorites:

- Place five candy corns on each person's plate before they sit down. Explain that the kernels represent what each Pilgrim's meal ration might have been during that first winter.

- Have a paper turkey cut from construction paper on the wall. Have each family member write what he or she is thankful for on a feather (made from paper) and attach it to the turkey.

- Make cornhusk dolls.

- Make quills from feathers. Make ink from boiled walnut shells.

- Make butter together: put heavy whipping cream in a jar along with one marble; seal and take turns shaking until the whey separates from the butter. Then use it at dinner.

- Have the children write a story from a Pilgrim's perspective.

- Listen to a radio drama of the story of Squanto (Focus on the Family has a great one).

- Make an acrostic poem from the word *Pilgrim* or *turkey* (or any other Thanksgiving word).

- Start a journal for Thanksgiving that will be added to each year. Have each person write what he or she is thankful for.

- Have the younger children create a book of what Thanksgiving means to them: cut out magazine pictures and glue to construction paper; tie the pages together with yarn.

- Have the older children write a pretend newspaper from the first Thanksgiving, complete with stories and "interviews."

- Playing games is a fun way to spend this day, especially if the games are old-fashioned ones.

- Make hoops with wire or pipe cleaners and use small sticks by which the hoop must be passed from person to person.

- Play the hot/cold game with a hidden picture of a turkey, but instead of saying "warmer" or "colder," gobble loudly or softly.

- Twenty questions is a great game to play: pick a topic related to Thanksgiving.

- And never underestimate the fun of a coloring contest. Use preprinted sheets to color or have children draw pictures freehand. The Internet is a great place to find coloring sheets if you prefer them preprinted. Two Web sites that offer several pictures are *www.kidsdomain.com/holiday/ thanks/color.html* and *www.coloring.ws/thanksgiving.html.* Do an Internet search using keywords like "Thanksgiving coloring pages."

EASTER

Easter is a time of celebration at our house. This is the day our Savior made our salvation possible by rising from the dead and leaving the tomb. Therefore, how we celebrate the day reflects that theme. But we incorporate traditional activities as well, like an egg hunt and spring crafts. Whatever you do to make this day special, our ideas should add something to your day.

Making Memories

There is so much we can learn and do to make the Easter season memorable. In addition to Easter, it is the celebration of spring, the time of Passover, and the end of Lent. We study Passover and the meaning of Lent throughout the Easter week, and even go back forty days to the beginning of Lent. Look for books at your church or public library (I have recommended my favorites at the end of this chapter). Some of the themes that we cover include:

- What the Passover rituals are and how they foretell of Jesus
- What Palm Sunday is and how people celebrate it
- What Good Friday is and why it is called "good"
- What Lent is, why it is observed, and why the first day of Lent is called Ash Wednesday

- What the day before Lent is called and why it is celebrated (Fat Tuesday or, in French, *Mardi Gras*)
- What a Seder service is, and attend one if possible

We make crafts that tell some of these stories. One of my favorites is an edible and fun activity that tells of the empty tomb. Take some biscuit dough that is cut into rounds and ready to bake. Place a marshmallow between two biscuit rounds and pinch the edges of the dough around the marshmallow so it is sealed inside. Bake the biscuits according to the directions. When they are done and you open them, the marshmallow is gone; there is a hollow space inside, but the biscuit remained sealed!

Another craft that kids enjoy is making salt dough (there is an easy recipe for it in chapter 29, "Crafts for Kids"). Let the kids make a tomb or complete garden surrounding the tomb. Let them put sticks in it for trees, toy soldiers, a door on the tomb (a rock or graham cracker will work), or anything else their imagination desires. We do this inside an empty shoebox.

My daughter's favorite activity for this time of year starts twelve days before Easter with our homemade version of Resurrection eggs. Resurrection eggs are a dozen plastic eggs housed in an egg carton, each filled with something to tell a part of the Easter story. In each egg we place something to remind us of the story along with a small piece of paper with a verse from the Bible that tells about that event. Once the eggs are completed, they can be stored for use each year or modified as you desire. There are many versions of the egg contents. Here are some to get you started:

- A plastic donkey for Jesus' entry into Jerusalem on Palm Sunday
- A piece of bread for the Last Supper

- Three dimes for the silver pieces given to Judas
- A nail for the nailing of Jesus to the cross
- A piece of fabric for the robe Jesus wore
- A small cross made of wood
- A piece of thorny flower stem for the crown of thorns
- A die for the casting of lots for His robe
- A rock for the tomb door
- A piece of gauze for the body wrappings
- Some whole cloves and cinnamon sticks for the spices that were brought to anoint the body
- A torn piece of cloth for the temple curtain that was torn

Discussing the origins of the Easter symbols is a fun activity. There are many ideas about where these traditions got started. Look up these ideas at the library: the egg symbolizes the new life that both spring and the resurrection give, the lily represents new life, the bunny symbolizes new life and spring, and the lamb symbolizes new life and meekness. An interesting tidbit of information we learned is how giving eggs on Easter got started: Eggs weren't allowed during Lent at one time, so people celebrated the end of Lent by giving and eating eggs.

Some other ideas that we enjoy are:

- Making Easter crafts: caterpillars from egg cartons, bird nests, paper chains, etc.
- Watching a movie together: *The Greatest Story Ever Told, The Robe, Jesus of Nazareth,* etc.
- Read some Easter stories together—some books are suggested at the end of the chapter.
- Study how other countries celebrate Easter.
- Attend a sunrise service on Easter morning.

- Take a nature walk and discuss the analogies that spring has with Christ's life.
- Write thank-you notes to those who have been helpful in bringing love and hope into your life.

Decorating

To help show the reason for Easter and decorate your home at the same time, create a display on a table near the entryway of your home. Have on it some symbols of Easter: a cross, a crown of thorns, a large nail, and/or a purple sash (hang it on the cross if desired). One family I know changes the scarf from purple to black on Good Friday, then from black to white on Easter morning.

Another project my children enjoy is creating a Jesse Tree with decorations of the different names for Jesus on it. We take a small tree branch and a flowerpot and spray-paint them gold. Then we place some foam in the center of the pot and place the branch in the center of the foam. We then cut hearts (about three inches wide) out of construction paper, write a name on each, punch a hole in the top of the heart, and tie a ribbon loop through it. Each day from Ash Wednesday to Easter we place one heart with one of the names for Jesus on the tree. This tree can also be placed on the entryway table with other Easter items.

VALENTINE'S DAY

We enjoy this holiday both as a family and as a special day for my husband and me. When I was young I thought this day should be a national holiday! It doesn't have to cost much to make it fun or romantic. It can be a special day to add to the family's memory bank, while costing pennies.

Decorating

A few simple touches can make this day special. Have the kids cut out paper hearts and decorate the house. Use different colors and types of paper (foil, lace, etc.). Make paper chains from red and white paper. Make a chain or wreath from valentines that you have received. We have found some great unopened Valentine's Day decorations at thrift stores too.

Making Memories

One of the things we do is study the origins of this day. We read about the saint called Valentine and why showing love is a feature of this day. You'll find several books in the library about this story.

Another one of my favorite things to do is to have my valentines re-mailed from America's Sweetheart City—Loveland, Colorado. For fifty-six years, Loveland has been offering its annual valentine's program to the public for free. Anyone can receive a unique stamp cancellation by placing the valentine that is to be mailed from Loveland in a stamped and addressed envelope, then inside a second envelope stamped and addressed to: Postmaster, ATTN: Valentine Re-mailing, 446 E. 29th St., Loveland, CO 80538-9998. Your valentine will be removed from the outer envelope and hand stamped with the Loveland cachet. To ensure that your valentine arrives by February 14, Loveland must receive it by February 9.

For your spouse, a touching gesture or gift will mean more than an expensive gift. Try some of these ideas:

- A nicely written list of all the reasons that you love and appreciate him or her. Go an extra step and *make* the paper that you write it on (see an easy recipe in chapter 29).
- Serve your loved one breakfast in bed.
- Cut out paper hearts and write love notes on them. Place

them throughout the house (and in his or her lunch box) so he or she will find them all day.

- Put a heart-shaped cookie in his or her lunch.

- Make a coupon book filled with ways to say "I love you" (a back rub, a foot rub, doing his or her chores for a day, etc.).

- Pull out your wedding album and look through it together.

- Listen to romantic music (classical, Tony Bennett, Frank Sinatra).

- Send an e-mail to each other letting the other know he or she is being thought about.

We also try to make this a special day for the entire family. Here are a few other ideas that we do to make it special:

- Have the kids make a box to store valentines in: take an empty Kleenex box and cover it with decorative paper (wrapping paper, contact paper, colored tissue paper, etc.).

- Talk as a family about giving an extra gift to a missionary or a local organization that helps the poor. Go together and give the money (if possible), accompanied by a valentine that you made together.

- Make heart-shaped cookies with the kids. Decorate them with red or pink icing.

- Make chocolate hearts-on-a-stick: Get inexpensive chocolate molds and sticks from a craft store, and pour melted chocolate into the molds. Before they harden insert the sticks.

- Make strawberry milk shakes (and any other pink food you can think of).

- Make festive ice cubes: Place candy hearts in ice-cube trays, fill with water, and freeze. Serve in the drinks at dinner.

- Study old-fashioned valentines and make one using doilies and construction paper.

- Bake a heart-shaped cake for the family dessert. Hide cinnamon candy hearts throughout the cake!

- Make valentine placemats and cover them with clear contact paper.

- Make coupon books for one another.

- Make bookmarks for one another. Glue paper hearts to construction paper and decorate them with markers or rubber-stamping. Cover in contact paper to preserve.

- Have a candy treasure hunt.

- Do a science project: Cut the base of the stem on a white carnation and put it in a glass of water that has red food coloring in it. In a few hours the flower will turn pink.

- Make an acrostic poem for someone with a valentine word: love, pink, red, heart, kiss, etc. Make each line something you like about that person.

- Watch a Charlie Brown movie together.

BIRTHDAYS

I keep birthday parties as simple as possible. A homemade cake, a few close friends, and a local city park usually are adequate. What kids enjoy most is playing with their friends and family. If more is desired, you can add simple games such as bubble wands, charades, homemade piñatas (paper-mache around a balloon), potato rolling with a spoon, or catching water balloons. You also can make the cake into an animal shape. There are several books on cake shape ideas at the library.

Another party idea is to let your child sleep in the backyard in a tent with a few buddies. Or have a pizza party—where they make the pizzas. Or have a bubble party. Make a huge amount of bubble solution (ten cups water to one cup Dawn or Joy—other brands don't bubble as well). Fill a wading pool with this. Hand out Hula-Hoops, and have the children stand in the hoop and pull a bubble around them. Hand out coffee cans that have both ends removed: they dip the opening in bubbles and blow out a huge bubble. Have them make their own wands by shaping coat hangers into shapes. (Closely supervise this, since the ends are sharp.) Once the shape is completed, duct-tape the ends.

If you like to give gift bags to the guests, scale those down too. Buy colored lunch sacks and let the kids decorate them with stickers and markers. Buy bulk candy or bulk tiny toys at warehouse clubs or party supply stores. Don't pay several dollars for each child's bag just because that's what is available at local stores.

If you'd like to go on an outing for the party, such as to the local zoo, take the lunch and cake along. Buying food and cake from the party location will cost significantly more—as much as four times.

There are numerous books in the library on fun, inexpensive birthday party ideas. My favorite is *Birthday Parties for Children: How to Give Them, How to Survive Them* by Jean Marzollo. It is full of age-appropriate party and game ideas that anyone can pull off.

As my kids become teens, their tastes in parties have changed. Sometimes teens don't want parties anymore. Some would prefer to go to the movies with one or two friends, or go miniature golfing. Mine prefer to go with one friend to an amusement park or a movie. I give them the budgeted amount I would have spent on a party. I usually am able to get discounted tickets to the park through organizations or stores that offer them at the beginning of each season. This leaves them enough money to buy food. Any extra purchases have to come from their own money.

There is no harm in limiting the size or expense of a birthday party. We don't get everything we want as adults; we shouldn't give our children the message that they can have whatever they want—especially if we can't afford it. That could get them into financial trouble later in life.

When you give a gift to another child, try to apply your miserly ways. I am not cheap in what I give, but I plan and watch for good prices. If I wait until the invitation arrives, I will likely have to run to the store and pay full price for a toy. One creative idea that a friend does is to buy wooden baking tool sets (rolling pin, small board, wooden spoon) when they are on sale during the "dollar days" events at her local grocery store. She buys several for future parties. When the time comes, she makes homemade scented play dough (see chapter 29, "Crafts for Kids") and wraps it with the baking set. This gift costs her two dollars. Another idea is to stock up on small toys when they are on sale and store them until needed. Don't give cash. You'll give more than you would spend on a toy.

-------------------------- *Resources* --------------------------

Benjamin's Box, Melody Carlson (Zondervan, 2000).

Birthday Parties for Children: How to Give Them, How to Survive Them, Jean Marzollo (Galahad Books, 2000).

Cake Decorating Bible, Anness Publishing Staff (Anness Publishing, Ltd., 2000).

Celebrating the Christian Year, Martha Zimmerman (Bethany House, 1993).

Christ in Easter, a Family Celebration of Holy Week, Chuck Colson, Billy Graham, Max Lucado (NavPress, 1990).

Family Fun Activity Book, Bob Keeshan (Deaconess Press, 1995).

A Family Guide to Biblical Holidays, Robin Sampson (Heart of Wisdom Publishing, 2001).

FamilyFun's Parties: 100 Party Plans for Birthdays, Holidays, and Every Day, Deanna Cook (Hyperion, 1998).

Free Family Fun and Super Cheap, Cynthia MacGregor (Replica Books, 2001).

Holiday Theme Parties: Entertaining Ideas, Decorations, and Recipes for Nine Unique Parties, Creative Publishing Staff (Creative Publishing, 2000).

"Thanksliving Box" (that's not a typo!), by FamilyLife Today, *www .familylife.com.*

www.party411.com. A Web site filled with party themes, budget planners, checklists, food, suggested gifts, decorations, and more.

CHAPTER 20

Baby Care

After sharing some tips on how to save money on baby necessities with my friend, she encouraged me to write a chapter on saving with babies. Here I cover all the expenses that caused a squeeze on our pocketbook when we had our babies.

DIAPERS

There is a never-ending debate over cloth versus disposable diapers. Some disagree with my math while others are convinced that the environmental impact of one over the other takes precedent. The debate over the environmental impact of disposable diapers versus the pollution caused by chemicals (ammonia or bleach) in the water system and from the extra utilities (wash and dry in hot water and hot dryer) is an interesting one if you choose to look into it.

Many of the off-brand disposable diaper brands are actually name-brand diapers that were relabeled for an off-brand company.

Aside from the environmental issue, there is the financial impact to evaluate. I compared the average cost of a hundred newborn-sized diapers. The most expensive alternative was a diaper service. It costs twice the amount of off-brand disposables or do-it-yourself cloth diapers. However, in my research I found that do-it-yourself cloth diapers cost almost the same as off-brand disposables. The difference was only a few dollars per month less for cloth diapers. The reason cloth diapers are not much cheaper is that many people forget to factor in *all* of the related expenses that go with cloth diapers: the high cost of the initial purchase of the cloth diapers, the diaper wraps, the propane or electricity to heat the hot-water washes, chemicals (ammonia or bleach), the extra laundry detergent, the extra fabric softener, and the electricity to heat the dryer. This adds up to quite a bit per load, and most families don't allow enough for that increase in expense. Most families add up to five extra loads of laundry per week to their normal laundry amount when they use cloth diapers. In some parts of the country the dryer alone costs over two dollars per load. Of course, if there are multiple children in the family, the cost of cloth diapers will get less and less, since the initial purchase only happens once or twice.

BABY FOOD

Sometimes we believe we need the products from the store shelves to properly care for our babies. But this is not always true. And making your own baby food can save you over two thousand dollars a year!

I found that if I mixed food I had cooked for dinner (minus the spices) with a few teaspoons of liquid in the blender, the food was as good as store-bought. This costs significantly less than a jar of pureed baby food—up to fifteen times less!

There are many types of grinders available to make the

food fine enough for the baby. If you don't have one, you can use your blender with good results. You don't need a special appliance for this. For meat, I boiled the beef or chicken until well done, put it in a blender, and added a bit of water, formula, or milk to provide a smooth consistency. Do the same with boiled vegetables. Adding milk or formula will provide extra protein where needed. For fruit, boiling helps make it soft enough to blend well.

I found I did not want to be grinding food every night while trying to prepare a meal for the family, so I learned to make my baby food in large portions. I stored it by freezing it in ice-cube trays. If I made a batch of chicken, I designated one tray for chicken. I made a tray of some type of vegetable, and another for fruit. I defrosted one square at a time, which is just the right size for a baby's meal.

THE EXPENSE OF FORMULA

Bottle-feeding with formula can be excessively expensive, adding up to a hundred dollars or more per month for one child. Formula can range in price, depending on whether it is powder, liquid, name brand, or hypoallergenic. But even when the cheapest type is purchased, the cost is still high.

Breastfeeding, on the other hand, is free. Even if a mother has to return to work after her maternity leave, pumping breast milk and storing it in the refrigerator to be used the next day is better on the pocketbook and the baby. I did this while I was still working after the birth of my first child.

Breastfeeding is the most cost-effective and healthy way to feed an infant. Studies have shown that the nutrients in breast milk are what babies need to develop their brains and bodies.

If a problem exists and the mother worries that her child isn't getting enough milk with breastfeeding, her doctor or her local La Leche League chapter (*www.lalecheleague.org*) can work with her to ensure her that the child is growing well.

BABY WIPES

By making these yourself, you can save a lot of money. I figure that a canister of homemade wipes costs less than a dollar. Aside from the container of wipes on the changing table, we carry a canister of them in the car for messy faces and fingers. I also refill my travel pack with them so I have some in my purse at all times.

Baby Wipes

> One roll of strong and thick paper toweling (I prefer Viva's ultra thick, 50-count)
> 2¼ C. water
> 2 T. baby shampoo (for sensitive skin use Mennen's Baby Bath)
> 1 T. baby oil
> 1 round plastic container, at least 6 inches high

Cut the roll of toweling in half (making 2 smaller rolls). Use a large cutting knife and sharpen it right before cutting and again during cutting. Do not use a serrated knife. Set aside one half of the roll for another day. Remove the cardboard tube by grabbing the edge of it with a pair of pliers and twisting as you pull. If the roll you have is too large for your container, pull some of the paper out with the tube so that it will compress to fit. Combine the wet ingredients in the container (before placing the toweling in), and set aside one cup of the mixture. Place the roll in the container (you may need to squeeze it a bit to fit). Pour the cup of liquid on top of the paper to saturate. Pull the wipes from the center of the roll.

BABY-SITTING

The cost of baby-sitting can make going out a rare occasion. Sometimes friends share the work by giving each other a day of the week off by trading kids. If a few moms form a baby-sitting co-op, everyone benefits. Most co-ops trade one-hour coupons instead of money for watching each other's kids. Each club varies on how they handle multiple children. Most common is to charge an extra coupon per hour, per child. To start a co-op, ask your friends and neighbors if they are interested. It only takes a few moms to get one started. Make coupons for one hour of sitting and start each member with a pack of ten (or whatever your group decides). Have a questionnaire for each member with basic questions: when is she not available; how does she feel about colds; does the family have pets, a pool, firearms, or other potential threats to a child's safety; is she willing to do overnights. These forms can then be copied for each member, allowing each mom to pick whomever she prefers to do the sitting.

TOYS

The cost of toys can be high. We try to keep the cost down by shopping good quality resale shops. We also shop the sales at toy stores. Each store has a clearance bin with some treasures in it. We have found twenty-five-dollar games for seven dollars. For a special item, we save and look for it on sale.

When the holidays are over and the New Year's Eve dishes are still sitting in the sink, your checkbook is probably in shock. The last thing you probably want to think about is more toys. But that is actually the best time to think about it. Toys and gifts are going to be on sale. Many stores want to clear out the excess inventory left after the holidays. Buy that toy that your child didn't get for Christmas and save it for his or her next birthday. Some of the best deals come from the warehouse clubs clearing out their excess toys.

If there is no conceivable way you can buy any more right now, don't panic. Many items go on sale a few times throughout the year. These are great times to buy for birthdays or even for the next Christmas.

When junior loses an important part of a toy, people tend to buy the whole toy to replace it. To save money—and toys—try contacting the manufacturer for that lost or broken piece. Most companies are very helpful and understanding. Here is a list of some of the major manufacturers to help you save your toys:

- Fisher-Price . . . . (800) 432-5437
- Lego Systems . . . . (800) 838-9647
- Little Tikes . . . . (800) 748-2204
- Playskool and Hasbro . . . . . . (800) 752-9755

Toy Containers

I was getting tired of all those little toys scattered on the floor or sitting in a pile in the kids' rooms. So I began reusing many of our containers as storage bins for those little things. I use oatmeal boxes, large yogurt containers, large plastic containers that bulk pretzels come in, and boxes. No need to buy that expensive container box the toy manufacturer wants you to believe you need.

Resources

Baby Bargains: Secrets to Saving 20 Percent to 50 Percent on Baby Furniture, Equipment, Clothes, Toys, Maternity Wear, and Much, Much More!, Denise and Alan Fields (Windsor Peak Press, 2007).

Super Baby Food, Ruth Yaron (F. J. Roberts Publishing, 1998).

CHAPTER 21

The Cost of Working

Working is very expensive. This may seem confusing to some, since most of us were raised to believe that if your expenses go up so must your income in order to compensate. Losing half of our income, however, helped us realize there were many hidden costs in working.

When I chose to stay at home with my children, we assumed we would have to move to a less expensive suburb to compensate for the 50 percent loss of income. But when I couldn't go through with the move, we were in a pickle: same house, same lifestyle, half the money. Even though I wanted to be at home full time, I looked at working part time out of desperation. Soon I realized how much working had cost me. Many expenses had surprisingly disappeared after I quit.

Financial experts have calculated the cost of working at anywhere from nine to thirty-five dollars per hour. I was stunned when I learned this! That meant that if I took a job paying ten dollars per hour, I might see only one dollar for every hour I worked.

Here are some of the expenses that went into these experts' calculations:

- child care
- taxes (local, federal, state)
- commuting fees (tolls, parking, etc.)
- gasoline and mileage
- car insurance (extra car, nicer car for the job, higher mileage, etc.)
- clothes (new clothes, accessories, etc.)
- gifts for co-workers
- fast-food lunches and breakfasts out
- convenience foods at home
- extra eating out
- occasional housekeeping help

Every person has a different cost of working. Some people have several children in child care, while others have no children. Some commute by car many miles to work; others ride a bike. Some can wear casual clothes to work, while others are required to dress in suits. Some pay more taxes than others. Use the list above to factor your cost of working.

After looking at my own experience, I soon realized that the experts' figures were accurate for me. I was spending nine to ten dollars per hour for the privilege of working.

When I stopped working, I spent less on clothes. Working sometimes requires special clothes. If not special ones, you need more outfits to rotate in your wardrobe than you do if you're at home. Then there is the cost of the accessories. Women, don't forget about the shoes and jewelry that need to match the outfits. For men, the cost of suits or dress slacks is high—not to mention the cost of dry cleaning. I discuss ways to reduce clothing expenses in chapter 22, "Clothing."

Aside from clothes, there is the cost of transportation and

parking. Some need a nicer car than they would if they were not working, one they can use for the transport of clients or co-workers. Some families might be able to eliminate one car if someone didn't work. The cost of wear on the car and tires, plus gasoline, comes close to fifty cents per mile (at the time of this writing). That's considerable when you see how many commuting miles you put on the car each day. Then there are the parking fees and added insurance for an extra car. In our area, insurance costs more if the car is used for commuting.

And then there is child care. The cost of child care can run from $350 to $900 per month per child. That's a lot of money. But I paid the money while I worked because I wanted the best for my child. Yet, even though the care was excellent, I still wanted to be with my child and see how he was doing. Perhaps we should add to the experts' list of expenses the cost of counseling from all of the worrying we do about our kids and the stress we encounter by working. After three and a half years, I didn't want to do it anymore.

We must not forget the portion due to Uncle Sam when we work. And remember that the more we earn, the more he takes. Most two-income families have a higher tax bracket than a single-income family. If one parent stops working, the tax deductions from the other spouse's salary may fall into a lower tax bracket. This can add up to a substantial amount of money. The point where it can make a difference is currently around $42,000 (joint income). Please consult a tax adviser to verify this for your family.

We must not overlook the savings we can achieve on the purchases we need to make. I am speaking of gifts for co-workers, relatives, household items, appliances, and even furniture. When we are working, we can't scour the sales and look for the best deals. We can't slowly acquire our Christmas and birthday gifts year round as we see a sale somewhere. I'm not saying that working folks don't shop around or look for good deals, but I am saying that they may be less able to watch for sales or visit several stores before making their purchases. When I was working, I sometimes had to settle for what seemed like a good deal because I had no time to go to several other stores to compare. Many people who work do make time for all of this shopping around, and they should be congratulated for their efforts. But they might be paying a higher price somewhere else, such as a lack of time with family members or hiring household help because their free time is spent elsewhere.

Another cost that many overlook is the additional food expense that working people incur. Working parents are very busy and very tired. They often forget or they don't want to make homemade lunches for themselves, so they eat out. Even if it's a cheap meal, it will run six to eight dollars. Most of us work twenty days per month, so lunches could cost you $160 per month. Then there's dinner to prepare when you get home. The working parent often relies on convenience meals or eating out because they don't want to cook from scratch, or there isn't enough time to wait for the food to cook. These conveniences cost up to six times more than a homemade meal. While my husband and I were both working (even part time for me), our food bill was four times higher.

Once I looked at these expenses that vanished when I quit, I decided to total them. Then I combined these savings with the ways I was going to further reduce our spending to see the overall savings of not working.

Here is a list of the categories in which we further reduced our spending:

(These figures are from 1991—just imagine what they would be like today!)

Category	Reduced By
Groceries	$250 per month
Not eating out	125 per month
Clothes	75 per month
Haircuts	60 per month
Automobile (gasoline and insurance)	50 per month
Medical insurance	25 per month
Cleaning supplies	10 per month
Total reduced spending	$595 per month

This amount combined with the loss of the "cost of working" makes for a healthy reduction in expenses.

Total reduced spending (from above)	$ 595 per month
My cost of working	$ 915 per month
Total saved by not working	$1,510 per month

$1,510 per month = $18,120 per year!

What this figure means to me is that if I returned to work, even part time, I would lose the first $18,000 of that salary to added expenses.

Many people are concerned that the time it takes to be thrifty doesn't make it worthwhile. This is not true. I figure that it takes me seven hours of thrifty work per week to make up what I was earning at my job.

Here is a breakdown of how that time is spent:

HOURS PER WEEK TO BE MISERLY

Task	Time
Shopping	2½ hours
Planning	½ hour
Shopping extra stores (bread store, warehouse clubs, super sale somewhere)	¾ hour
Extra cooking (homemade syrup, granola, relishes, snacks, etc.)	3 hours
Total	7 hours per week

CHAPTER 22

Clothing

I spend about five hundred dollars per year on clothes for a family of four. The average American family spends more than $1,800 per year (according to the Bureau of Labor Statistics). My family's clothes look nice—no stains and tears. In order to spend this little, we must plan what our clothing needs will be and shop carefully. I figure out how many outfits, dresses, men's slacks, etc., we need each month or two, then I look for the best prices on these items. If I shopped at department stores without planning, I would probably spend two hundred dollars every time.

My annual total includes dress slacks—but not suits—for my husband. When I buy slacks for him, I try to avoid those that require dry cleaning, as this expense adds up quickly. If suits are required for your husband's job, watch for sales at department stores and purchase two pairs of slacks for each jacket, since slacks wear out faster. Buy neutral-colored pants and/or jackets so as to match future purchases.

If buying new clothes is a hardship but you want your children to look nice, these are some good alternatives: I have found many great bargains at the "rerun" stores throughout our area. There are the big-name places such as Savers, Salvation Army, and Goodwill. Then there are the independent thrift stores in each city. Some of the wealthier neighborhoods might have a better selection of clothing to offer. Finding clothes may take some time, as the items come and go weekly.

There are also the seasonal resale stores (in our area there is one called Outrageous Outgrown), where a few well-organized women set up a store for a few days through which we can each sell our clothes, toys, etc., at prices we choose. Another idea that has helped many families here is to organize a clothing exchange. On a designated weekend, people bring in their used clothing and then take what they need from the selection. One day is for dropping off and the other is for "shopping." It's a great way to help each other out and to go home with newfound treasures. Ask your church or local community center to sponsor it. Each of these situations offers some great clothes at great prices.

If you prefer to buy new clothes, the best way is to watch sale flyers and stock up when prices are very low. One friend taught me to save even more by buying clothes one size too large for the children, and then loosely sewing the sleeve of a shirt into the cuff or a blouse sleeve into the shoulder seam and hemming the pants or skirts. When the kids grow, simply let out these allowances.

Garage sales and local flea markets have a lot of variety. When you see one with children's clothes and toys, stop and investigate. Again, the wealthier the neighborhood, the better the selection of items. I have found nice sweaters for a dime and good toys for one-tenth their value.

Buy used clothing at consignment shops or used-clothing stores that offer top-quality brand-name clothing. No clothes are accepted that are worn or stained. You can save 50 percent off what you'd pay for retail.

Watch for sales at the discount clothing stores such as Ross, Dress for Less, or Marshalls. Many stores clear out fashions or seasonal clothes at 40 to 50 percent off. Stock up. Adults usually aren't growing anymore, so you can buy for next year with pretty good confidence that the clothes will fit. Check out their prices on socks and other accessories; they might be on sale as well.

Avoid the so-called sales at the big-name department stores. The bigger-name stores have inflated prices and then have 40- to 50-percent-off "sales" to lure you in. Compare their prices to the discount department stores.

 *Resources*

Cash for Your Used Clothing, William R. Lewis (Client Valuation Services, 2000).

Secondhand Chic: Finding Fabulous Fashion at Consignment, Vintage, and Thrift Stores, Christa Weil (Pocket Books, 1999).

CHAPTER 23

Help for the Working Mom

In preaching the value of not working outside your home, I don't want to overlook the working mom. Many women truly must work, and perhaps you are one of them. You may have squeezed every penny you can from the budget, but it still isn't enough. Maybe you have had an unexpected emergency or another high expense your budget cannot absorb. You might be a single-income parent. Or perhaps you do not have any children and enjoy working, but you need help with your budget. Whatever the reason, this chapter is dedicated to helping the working woman stretch her dollar.

As I discussed earlier, the expense with the largest opportunity for savings is groceries. After reviewing the eleven guidelines, I have summarized how working moms can apply them and make the best use of their limited time.

GROCERIES

You can still put a major dent in your food bill, but you will need to approach shopping and cooking differently. Most of the eleven guidelines can apply to the working mom, but the following are the best use of her time.

1. *Plan your menus around the sale flyers*

I cannot stress this point enough. This one step alone can cut your grocery bill by 30 percent. If you only have time for one trip to the store, make it work for you. Don't just drop in and buy what you need. Plan around the store's sales. Use their loss leaders as your basis for all meals, snacks, and produce.

2. *Stock up on sale items*

When your local store mails out a coupon book, use it. Go there only once each month and buy those things you generally use. Don't let low prices tempt you into buying things you wouldn't normally buy. Stock up on the things you regularly use, and buy enough to last you six weeks. That's when another coupon book will come out.

3. *Avoid convenience foods*

It's so easy to depend on prepackaged foods, mixes, and frozen meals when you are busy working. But you pay for that ease. Most of those items cost four to six times more than a homemade version of the same thing. To make the most of your time, find the things you are paying the most for and replace them with homemade. If these are snacks and lunchbox items, then make alternatives for those.

4. *Avoid eating out*

Make your own sack lunch. Those cafeteria and fast-food lunches add up. Avoid the vending machines, even for a soft drink. They charge three times more than you need to pay. Take a reusable bottle full of juice or a six-pack of soda and leave it in the office refrigerator. Don't grab coffee or breakfast at a restaurant or cafeteria on the way to work. Fill the coffeemaker the night before and flip the switch on your way to the shower in the morning. Grab a banana and toast if you're late. You'll save!

5. *Do your shopping and cooking once a month*

If you are working you may not have the time to go to three or more stores per week to get foods at the lowest prices. If you can't take full advantage of the loss leaders at several local stores, buying in bulk is your next best option. Shop the good deals when you can, buying enough for the month's meals. For example, buy chicken when it's on sale. And buy enough for the month.

With all this bulk food, you should then set aside one or two days per month to cook—part of a weekend works well. Prepare the month's meals and freeze them. Some people shop throughout the month for sales, then cook on a Friday night and a Saturday morning.

With this plan you will save money and time by:

- buying in bulk (lower costs)
- keeping homemade "convenience" meals in the freezer (reduces eating out)
- spending less time each evening cooking and washing pots and pans

CLOTHES

To combat the high cost of a work wardrobe, you must look at the styles you wear, where you buy them, and how you clean them.

As for the styles you wear, avoid trendy fashions. Don't buy anything that can only be worn alone, such as a fancy shirt or patterned dress. Stick with classic designs and colors that can be mixed and matched and that will still be in style five years from now. I buy neutral-colored shirts that can be worn with any neutral skirt or slacks. They can be combined with other neutral jackets or skirts for a completely different outfit. If I spent the same amount on a dress, I could only wear it once in a while, as opposed to several times with the mix-and-match approach. The same goes for shoes. Don't buy red shoes for the red dress. You can only wear them with that outfit. Buy neutral colors (brown, tan, navy, gray, black) and wear them with all the outfits. Remember, you aren't running for fashion queen. You're trying to keep your money for your family.

Pick fabrics that can be hand- or machine-washed. The dry cleaners take a big chunk out of your budget. Buy lighter-weight fabrics that can be worn in layers when it's colder and alone when warm.

For underwear and pantyhose, buy in bulk from the manufacturers. Many have outlet stores in the malls. Most offer catalogs. Many have frequent-shopper cards that let you earn free purchases after a certain amount is spent. Buy their irregular or imperfect pairs to save even more. I have saved another 50 percent by buying irregulars. These have minor flaws. I have never had problems with them. Wash pantyhose by hand and rinse in fabric softener to help them last longer.

Resources

The Complete Financial Guide for Single Parents, Larry Burkett (Victor Press, 1992).

The Working Mom's Book of Hints, Tips, and Everyday Wisdom, Louise Lague (Peterson's, 1995).

CHAPTER 24

Getting the Husband Involved

When talking with a few friends about their budgets, one had a great question: How do you get your husband committed? Not committed to an asylum; committed to a budget and your miserly ways.

This may prove to be one of the harder parts of the miserly lifestyle. If you are pinching the copper from every penny but your husband eats out for lunch every day, you have a hole in the budget bag.

After the birth of our second child, I was too tired to shop. I sent my dear husband to the store with a list. He was not interested in my method of shopping at a few stores and only buying sale items. He went to one store and bought everything. He spent twice what we usually did for one week of groceries (the salsa and chips helped increase the bill). I realized then that he needed to be convinced of the payoff in my method of shopping and the importance of my goal.

In order to get my husband to agree to the other spending changes I wanted to try, I needed to convince him that those changes would be easy and profitable. Men tend to want to see numbers on paper to help them understand. Many men think all you're doing is saving a few cents here and there. As you know, it's much more than that.

The best thing I did to convince my husband was to annualize the savings we could achieve. By reducing expenses and applying my guidelines to our groceries, I showed him I could save $7,140 per year from our current budget. By quitting my job, I could reduce other hidden expenses by another $10,980 per year. By doing both (quitting and applying miserly ways), I was saving our family more than $18,000 per year. I asked him what he could do with an extra $18,000. (These figures were in 1991.)

The other thing that impressed my husband was the first major purchase made with the savings I had accumulated. After two months of miserly shopping and cooking, I had set aside enough money to buy six oak dining room chairs. That spoke to him.

Another thing that helped convince him this was all worth the trouble was when I explained that it doesn't take that much time. It takes about seven hours per week to apply the things I have learned.

If all else fails, try to make a deal with him. Ask him how much he thinks he needs to spend each week (lunches, magazines, etc.). Then ask him if he would take that amount in cash and leave the rest to you. Then you can be a thrifty person in shopping, cooking, and other household expenses and show him how much you saved (cash speaks loudest) at the end of two to three months. If he enjoys eating lunch out, ask him if he'd take a sack lunch to work instead. Show him how much his lunches out are costing the family. Promise him you will make his lunch a tasty meal.

Another way to stop major leaks in a budget is an agreement that neither of you will buy anything over a certain amount (agree on that amount) without consulting your spouse. This policy doesn't apply to any "mad money" you each get as an allowance. You can spend that where you like without anyone's opinion. It's those trips to the department stores or the mall that get us into spending trouble. It's that cute outfit in the catalog, or a nice kid selling stuff to raise money for school. By having to discuss it, it gives you time to reflect on whether you really need it and to compare the price to somewhere else. It also curbs the impulse buying that manufacturers hope we will succumb to.

Many husbands (like us wives) have certain weak spots where they spend freely. My husband's weak spot was books. He could drop a hundred dollars a month in books. He justified it because they were reference or research books and not junk. I needed to help him find an alternative way to satisfy this urge, or our financial ship was going to sink. We learned how the inter-library loan system worked. Your library can access almost any library in the U.S. We were amazed that you can check out any book you need with a free card. Even if the book is new, you can request it be purchased or borrowed from another library. We also discovered we could borrow movies and CDs for free. This helped plug that hole in the ship. Be creative with any trouble spots your family has with money.

If all of these ideas still sound nuts, try writing down everything you spend for one month. Then categorize what you spent (entertainment, food, subscriptions, clothes, household, hobbies, bank fees for overdraft charges, etc.) and figure the total for each category. See how much was wasted on trivia. Show your husband the damage. Also ask him how important it is to him to have his children raised by strangers through child care, or by his wife for a few sacrifices. He might become a convert.

CHAPTER 25

Ten Ways to Get Kids to Save

While shopping, it is very easy to give in to a child's persistent whining about a toy or special treat, especially when you are holding a screaming baby, a toddler, a shopping list, and a diaper bag. It's easier to grab what is convenient or familiar and get out of the store as fast as possible.

These are the times when your miserly skills are tested severely. The best way to solve this weekly battle is to get your kids on your side. Help them to see the finances your way. Then you can reinforce what you've explained while shopping. Let me clarify. If junior understands there is a limited amount of money to be spent at the store, then he will say "Oh yeah!" when you remind him you can't afford that impulse item or a more expensive brand of cereal.

It's hard to get them to understand that there is a limit to the green stuff when they see the cash machines spitting it out whenever we punch some buttons. My kids used to say, "What do you mean we don't have any more money? Just go to the bank machine or write a check."

Here are some tips that have helped my kids become involved:

1. *Shop alone as often as possible.*

This, of course, is the ideal situation. You can compare prices as you need to and stop whenever you want to, regardless of what toys are in front of you (why do you think those toys are placed at their eye level?). And most important, you can think. But reality is something different. During school hours there may be fewer kids in your shopping cart. Try shopping then.

2. *Explain that you have a limited amount of money and choices have to be made.*

Explain the concept of a budget, and that plans have been made for all the money the family has. Use a pie chart with colors for each budget category. Exact numbers are not necessary to get the point across. Even five-year-olds can understand that there are basic limits.

3. *While at a store, explain what amount you plan to spend at this particular store.*

If they are used to seeing you buy whatever you want when you go shopping, then they won't understand why they can't do the same. Let them see you put some things back when you realize you are spending beyond your budget.

4. *Give them the facts: "I can't afford it."*

Who says they should have everything they want? They are never too young to learn this principle.

5. *Ask them if they want to use their allowance to buy it.*

When faced with the decision of whether or not to spend their own money, they quickly realize its value.

6. *Use the opportunity to help them learn to make choices.*

Explain that if you buy a brand of cereal with the fancy toy inside instead of the generic one, the difference will prevent you from doing something else (a movie rental or an outing of the same value) or buying some other food they want. Let them make the choice and then hold them to it.

7. *For the very persistent (and young), let them pick one item that isn't budgeted.*

Give them a small amount of money (one to two dollars) that they can spend. This will keep them busy while you shop: they will switch and trade, keeping out of your way. All other wants have to be traded for that one, so when you get to the cash register, their purchase is no more than their given amount.

8. *When you are away from the store, let them see or learn about other economic lifestyles.*

Let them see you donate some of your income to help others. Explain how you planned for that donation in the budget. Take them with you to a homeless shelter or rescue mission to help serve food. Help them to learn about other cultures and our abundance.

9. *If there is a certain item they always ask for, show them how the system works.*

Let them watch for sales and coupons in the grocery store flyers and Sunday coupons. My son loves a certain brand of ice cream that is very expensive. I normally don't buy ice cream unless it's a great sale or I have a wonderful coupon. One day I found him on the floor going through the Sunday newspaper coupons. He found a great coupon for that brand of ice cream, and he also saw that it was on sale at a local store. Eureka! At last he understands! (And he got the ice cream.)

10. *For those larger-ticket items, I have found two ways to tame them.*

First, I tell them to add the item to their Christmas or birthday list. I explain that most relatives enjoy getting a special item for them on a special occasion.

If they can't wait that long, I have them save their allowance for big-ticket items. If it's very expensive and special, I might match what they save.

Making a list of jobs for money around the home is also an incentive to earn the item faster. If they aren't interested in working for the item, then it must not be that important to them.

From these suggestions, I hope to teach my kids the value of money and patience. We will be constantly challenged. It's worth it to stick to your guns during those hard times. They need to learn that love should not be measured by money.

HOW TO SAVE WITH TEENAGERS

Someone said that my grocery spending goal was nice, but I must not have any teenagers in the house. She was right. I didn't have teenagers in the house when I first wrote this book. But I do now! And we are still able to keep our food bill within our goals. And I have several friends who have teenagers and are able to keep their food bill down to forty dollars per week. The only way that is possible is to cook from scratch, avoid those convenient snack foods, and cook in bulk. Aside from those tips, here are a few others that pertain to saving with teenagers.

Food

- Watch the snacks! Snack foods and teenagers can be a costly combination. Make snacks once per month and keep on hand: cookies, muffins, breads, pizza, drinks, etc.

- If you can't make something very well (such as potato chips), stock up when they go on sale.

- Ask teens to use some of their own money for those non-essential snack foods.

Name-Brand Clothes

- Give them their allotted clothes money, which would pay for good off-brand clothes on sale.
- Let them make up the difference for name-brand clothes by using their allowance and job money.
- Show them how to shop for their name-brand items at good resale, consignment, and thrift shops.
- Start assigning certain expenses to them (clothes, gas, cosmetics, entertainment, etc.)

It's better for teens to learn how to budget and experience mistakes while at home than to get into debt after they move out on their own.

Resources

Raising Money Smart Kids: What They Need to Know About Money and How to Tell Them, Janet Bodnar (Kiplinger's Personal Finance, 2005).

The Totally Awesome Money Book for Kids and Their Parents, Bochner & Berg (Newmarket, 2007).

CHAPTER 26

Five Things I Wish I Knew About Money When I Was Younger

Hindsight is such a powerful thing. We look back with wisdom and say, "I wish I had done that differently." Wouldn't it be cool to look forward to avoid some obstacles that can derail us?

When I asked several people what they wish they had known about money when they were young, these were their most common answers.

1. *I wish I had known how to use a credit card.*

Our mailboxes get filled with credit card offers. To the inexperienced person, that seems like Christmas! To a college graduate with little money, it appears to be a lifesaver. But it's not "free money" and might be an anchor around their neck if unwisely used.

Most of us get the card, then spend, spend, and spend some more. Then we get the bill and can't pay it. We can manage the minimum monthly amount, but the finance charges keep canceling out those payments, leaving us spinning our financial wheels. Just because you can afford the monthly payments doesn't mean it's okay to use the card. If the average person made only the minimum payments on their current credit cards and stopped charging to them, it would take around thirty years to pay them off. Another way to look at it is, the $15,000 loan may cost you $30,000 over time with all the interest you end up paying.

Some financial teachers advocate having zero debt and never using credit cards. I take a more moderate stance than they do. Don't go overboard by treating credit like the plague. I have seen students of these teachers avoid credit to such an extreme that they ask others for help to pay for their purchases just to avoid getting a loan. But if you are a credit addict and have no self-discipline, then avoid credit cards altogether as they suggest. My advice is to let the credit be your tool, and not let the bank make you a tool.

The flip side to this problem is that we need to use *some* credit. Having a credit history is essential today. Unless you plan on paying cash for everything and never getting a loan for a home or car, you will need a good credit history. To build a credit history, one needs to have a credit card and show the banks they can use it wisely. The best way to do that is to use the card for a small purchase and pay it off in a few regular monthly installments, then stop using the card. That takes self discipline, but it's worth it!

If you have some self-discipline but just need to know how to navigate the credit road, then use the credit card as a tool. Many banks are offering rebates of some sort in order to get you to use their card. If you can use the card and pay it off in a timely manner, then use the rebate programs for your benefit. But if you are weak at controlling your spending, then don't try what I am about to suggest. There are such a variety of rebate types that you can get one that works for you. There are cash-back programs, free groceries, free gasoline, and free airline miles, just to name a few. I really enjoy my rebate gasoline card, since it gives me 5 percent back on all gasoline purchases from a specific brand of gas. But the one that we really scored on was the airline miles. We were able to fly to Hawaii for free by running all of our monthly expenses through the card and paying them off at the end of each month—we just had to keep track of the spending just like it was a checkbook we were using. Look for double point offers to help add things up faster.

Lesson learned: Use money like a tool and don't get fooled by the lure of "free" money.

2. I wish I had taken care of my teeth.

This may seem odd to include in the money section, but repairing teeth and spending money go together very well. I have too many friends and relatives who have had to spend thousands of dollars each year replacing or repairing teeth; they could have prevented this by taking care of them in the first place. Sadly, most of us ignore the dental advice, thinking we are young and invincible (not to mention it's uncool to floss daily). It pays to listen to your dentist's advice.

Lesson learned: A little bit of prevention can save a lot of money.

3. I wish I had invested money early—even if it was just a tiny bit.

The power of compounding interest is enormous. A small monthly investment left to grow over the years can yield a small fortune. When we are young, we are usually barely able to meet our monthly obligations. But if we could put as little as $10 to $20 away each month into a compounding interest account, many of our future financial needs would be met. As we get older, we can add to that monthly amount and increase the return.

To show an example, let's take a man who waits until he is forty to begin investing $100 per month. His compounding account will yield $41,663 by age sixty (at 5 percent interest). But if he had put away $100 per month starting at age twenty, he would have had $152,207 at age sixty.

Every time we have a bit of extra income, we spend it. If we get a raise, we figure out what else we can spend it on. Wouldn't it be great if we let it roll into savings for a rainy-day expense? Try to live without the raise or extra money just like you did before you had it. Save it.

Lesson learned: Every little bit helps, so make it happen.

4. *I wish I had learned the importance of postponing purchases.*

The media saturates us with the message that we should have all this stuff and great vacations, and that somehow it's our right to have them whenever we want them. Sadly, that message is drowning out the message our parents tried to teach us, which was to wait until we could afford it.

I remember not having a TV for a while; going camping for vacation because that's all we could afford; being told we couldn't afford that toy, and I should save up for it if I wanted it. We need to go back to those lessons and live without things that we can't afford. There is no shame in it.

Even after twenty or more years of practicing frugality and teaching others about spending control, I still have to ask myself why I want to buy that thing. Do I really need it or do I just want it? Am I spending emotionally and need to fill some need that material things have no place filling? Am I spending recreationally? We never stop being challenged with materialism.

Psychologists have even learned that owning too many things actually can cause depression and anxiety. How ironic when we often buy things to make us feel better, safer, and more secure. For those who buy things to achieve a certain status, researchers have found that those things quickly lose their value. This type of buyer is often angry and anxious, going from false value-filler to false value-filler. Other researchers have found that the clutter of items in our homes causes a sense of anxiety and distraction or focus problems. Having clutter can often lead to feelings of being overwhelmed (it's too much stuff to tackle so it just grows). That can lead to a feeling of loss of control and anxiety. Also, having stuff catch your eye everywhere you turn can cause focus and attention problems. And finally, all that stuff cost you a lot. Are you still paying off those purchases? What else could you have done with that money?

Lesson learned: Delayed gratification is okay, despite what the marketplace tells you.

5. I wish I knew earlier that building relationships was just as important as building work skills.

Neither work skills nor relational skills are more important than the other; both are essential. I have seen too many people who stressed their work skills to the exclusion of their relational skills, believing they were achieving success. Many went as far as justifying this choice and neglect by saying they were doing it for the family. How ironic when the family really would like the relational side as well.

On the flip side, I have seen people who rely only on their relational skills and spend no time on their job skills. These people slide by for a time, but their lack of skill will catch up with them. We need both sides.

Some researchers have said that career success is only 15 percent skill and 85 percent personality and relationships. I wish I had known that earlier. I was very successful in my jobs but neglected the relational aspect. It wasn't until I was older that I realized this imbalance and began to work on it. The ones who succeed in their careers are the ones who get along well with others, are not prone to mood swings, are supportive of their bosses, are trustworthy and have integrity, and are well liked.

Lesson learned: Don't neglect relationships for grades or skills, and don't neglect skills for relationships.

CHAPTER 27

Medical Expenses and Insurance

Nothing can wipe out your savings, current assets, and future plans faster than an uninsured medical situation. This can throw your plans for retirement, savings, and even home ownership into chaos. It's not worth the risk.

I know of a family who said they couldn't afford medical insurance, so they didn't buy any. They weren't poor and had money for other items some might consider nonessential. The mother of this family had a freak accident and needed hundreds of thousands of dollars in care and surgeries. They asked friends to help bail them out because they hadn't taken some basic steps to insure themselves.

Please remember that the advice I share is lay advice and should never be substituted for any professional health-care advice.

MEDICAL INSURANCE

Many people make a superficial decision when choosing an insurance carrier. Some choose one type of plan simply because they prefer the ease of a co-payment rather than submitting an insurance bill for a refund. The decision for our care should go beyond convenience. We should look at the type of care we'll receive as well as the annual cost differences between carriers.

The first thing to remember is that you need insurance. Many families I know don't have it because they are mostly healthy or they can't afford it. But just one accident or illness could wipe them out or have them at other people's doors asking for financial help. Another reason to carry it is that you will always be treated better if you have insurance. Many doctors and hospitals won't provide care or will provide it with less quality and attention than for insured patients.

If you are fortunate enough to be able to shop for insurance, ask yourself these questions: What type of care do I want? Is it important to me to have a doctor I know and that I can see each time I need to? Will I get the best testing done for a problem I encounter? Can I go where I think I need to? The answers to these will direct you to the type of carrier you should choose. An HMO (Health Maintenance Organization) will provide you with "managed" care. This means that the doctors (and not you) decide when you need further tests, and they decide who does them. Some HMOs are more controlling than others, not allowing you to see the doctor of your choice. Some allow you to select the doctor of your choice, but then require that you stay within his/her clinic for all other medical needs. The thing to remember about this type of insurance carrier is that the more control they have over your care, the lower your medical premium will be. This is because they decide what care you get, and they save money if they provide less care.

We have switched insurance providers a few times over the years. We usually did this for cost reduction: switching insurance companies, but keeping our doctor, to reduce our premiums and overall out-of-pocket expenditures. When we switched to a more expensive carrier, our monthly premiums went up, but the overall out-of-pocket expenditures were less.

We made this change when we discovered that my husband had cancer. We had caught it at an early stage and had the freedom to wait six months to begin treatment. We decided to use that time to get him as healthy as possible with diet and exercise. We also used that time to wait for the next insurance open-enrollment period through his employer. That allowed us to switch to an indemnity insurance carrier—one that allows you to see any doctor you want while you pay an annual deductible, plus 30 percent of the bill. We wanted the freedom to go anywhere we wished. There was a fairly new treatment for his type of cancer that the local doctors didn't know how to perform. The option that was available locally was invasive and carried more severe side effects. The option we wanted to pursue was available out-of-state. If we had not waited to change carriers, we would have been limited to our town's HMO plan and their treatment options. Sometimes paying a higher monthly premium pays in the long run.

After you decide which type of insurance is right for you and your family, you should then start doing some comparative shopping. The most accessible and the cheapest place to buy insurance is through your employer or your spouse's employer.

If you have no employer policy available, look at any professional groups that you belong to: your college's alumni association, your automobile insurance carrier, or any school you may be attending. Buying a policy as an individual will cost you 15 to 40 percent more than with a group. There are also companies such as Blue Cross Blue Shield that sell directly to individuals. There are groups of people who form their own insurance group by pooling their money. The families accepted must all adhere to certain lifestyles and health requirements (such as no smoking, drinking, drugs) to participate.

When you purchase medical insurance, estimate what your medical needs will be during the next year. List what you needed last year. Then consider things such as the types of hospital services you may need, surgeries, prescriptions, ambulance, well-baby care, maternity, physical therapy, out-of-town coverage, chronic illness coverage, and any annual cap on what you will spend. Then factor in the potential carrier's portion. By doing this sort of evaluation, we saved three hundred dollars per year.

Once you have selected a carrier, find out about their policy on visits to urgent care facilities and emergency rooms. One type of service might be covered at a very different rate than the other. Also some carriers restrict the coverage of certain types of visits to urgent care facilities and emergency rooms and might even refuse to pay.

A few more things to remember when choosing insurance:

MEDICAL INSURANCE TIPS

Don't always assume that cheaper is better. Check out the reputation of the carrier and make sure the company has a high rating. See how A.M. Best Company rates them (*http://www3.ambest.com/ratings/default.asp*).

Don't under-insure yourself or your family. Make sure you will be covered for major things.

Pay as high a deductible as you can afford. You only want to pay for coverage of losses that you can't afford. The higher the deductible, the lower the payments.

HOSPITALS

Most people assume that a doctor or hospital bill is a fixed fee. In many cases it is, but not always. Many doctors are very understanding and will accept whatever the insurance company will cover combined with whatever you are able to pay. Many large bills can be negotiated, especially if the hospital is in a lower-income area. These hospitals have many customers who simply can't pay for their visits, so the hospital has to write off the cost. If a customer can pay but needs to make small payments, they usually cooperate in order to get the money eventually.

My husband had to spend three days in intensive care at a hospital in a lower-income part of a city. When all of the various bills arrived (there were twelve in all), we could only afford to pay each at ten dollars per month. All of them (except the hospital) were willing to accept these terms, and none ever charged interest.

On a separate trip to a hospital a few years later, we landed in a wealthier part of town. This four-hour hospital stay cost more than our three-day visit to intensive care at the other hospital. This hospital did not want to accept payments. Instead, they offered us a 20-percent discount if we paid by the end of that month. That added up to a large savings and was worth doing what we had to in order to pay it.

Don't be afraid to contest the amount that the insurance company decides to cover. There are people with tender hearts working at these companies. I have had medications and procedures covered that normally would not be because I wrote a sincere and explanatory letter regarding the situation. Send supporting documents, such as a doctor's letter, if you can.

DOCTOR BILLS

When you use your insurance, find ways to reduce the expense of the bill. Use the carrier's preferred doctors and save 40 percent. Ask the carrier how else you can reduce your part of the bill. Some doctors will write off your portion of the bill if you show financial need.

Use the phone for a consultation as often as possible instead of making an appointment. Many doctors will advise you over the phone. You can save sixty dollars or more by letting your fingers do the walking.

Check out what your local county board of health has to offer. Many offer immunizations for children for free or for a minimal fee of five dollars. A visit to the doctor for the same service runs seventy-five dollars or more.

MEDICATIONS

When buying prescription or over-the-counter drugs, go for the generic version as often as possible. This can save you 30 to 80 percent compared with the cost of its name-brand equivalent. And even generic or store-brand versions of the same drug can vary greatly in price. One store's own brand of aspirin may be much cheaper than another store's. Comparing prices is essential. And don't fear the quality. There are strict controls on the production of medications, so one brand has to be made exactly like another in order to be called by the same chemical name (e.g., ibuprofen). The only time to be concerned about buying a generic version is if the store is a "dollar store" or the chain is small or independently owned. Often, the disreputable manufacturers sell their lots of look-alike drugs to stores that don't verify their source. These look-alikes have sometimes been made of plaster and packaged to look like the name brand, or they come from a country with unregulated manufacturing standards so the doses vary from pill to pill.

Don't overlook mail-order pharmacies. These are great for medications you use regularly. They can give a good discount: up to 60 percent off name-brand prescriptions. If you have access to Costco, they offer a prescription drug plan only for those without drug insurance. Their prices are very low compared to full retail; it's worth talking to them about it.

For those who have no prescription insurance plan, there is a program that might help. Most major drug manufacturers offer drugs for little or no fee to those who cannot afford to purchase them. Each company has different requirements for receiving free prescription drugs, but all require a doctor's application on your behalf. If your doctor is unfamiliar with the program, have him/her contact the Pharmaceutical Research and Manufacturers of America at (202) 835-3400 or *www.phrma.org*.

When one of us has a cold, I avoid the combination remedies. There is usually some drug in there we don't need, and they tend to be more expensive than the individual ingredients combined—as much as 20 to 30 percent more. Any time you buy medicine, compare the unit price (the cost per milliliter or milligram). Sometimes it's cheaper to take two capsules of a smaller dose

---

GENERIC NAMES & PURPOSES FOR COLD MEDICATIONS

Dextromethorphan: for dry cough/ cough suppressant

Guaifenesin: for productive or "gooey" cough/expectorant

Pseudoephedrine: decongestant

Ephedrine: decongestant

Chlorpheniramine: antihistamine

Diphenhydramine: antihistamine

---

than to take one of a larger dose. This is particularly true of aspirin and other painkillers.

We keep several separate drugs in the cabinet—one for each type of symptom. When I have a particular symptom, I take only the drug appropriate for that symptom. Some people like the hot flu medication drink that is packaged for your convenience. Instead, take what you need (fever reducer, decongestant, antihistamine) and have a hot cup of herb tea or hot water with lemon juice and honey. The same effect will be achieved and it will cost you much less. See the sidebar for a list of drugs and their indicated purpose. This should make shopping for the right remedy a bit easier and help you avoid taking drugs you don't need.

It's important to know what you need. You can complicate your problems by using the wrong drug. For example, if you have a productive (phlegmy) cough, using a cough suppressant isn't a good idea. Ask your doctor or pharmacist before you self-medicate to be sure you're choosing the right medicine.

When shopping for vitamins, the same guidelines apply. Know what elements you need and shop around for the best generic price. Don't forget to check the expiration dates as well. To know if you are getting a good manufacturer of the tablet, try this quick test: Drop a tablet in a few teaspoons of any kind of vinegar (to simulate stomach acid) and leave it for forty-five minutes (you can stir it once in a while to simulate stomach churning). It should break apart or dissolve by the end of the experiment. If it doesn't, then the manufacturer packs it too tightly or adds too many fillers, and it passes through you unabsorbed. I tested all of my vitamins and found one of mine that didn't dissolve. All the time that I took them, I wasn't getting any benefit from them. I wrote to the manufacturer and received a full refund. If you would like to know which brands of multivitamins are more complete, check the library for recent articles that review the most popular brands of vitamins.

DENTAL EXPENSES

The best way to avoid dental work is to take care of your teeth: brush, floss, avoid sweets, and have regular cleanings and exams. Thirty-five percent of all gum disease and tooth loss is caused by plaque. A root canal can cost hundreds of dollars per tooth. You can buy a lot of dental floss, toothpaste, and toothbrushes for that kind of money.

Dental schools offer low-cost cleanings, exams, and dental work. They charge 50 to 75 percent less than a private dentist. Certified dentists always supervise the students. If you cannot afford any amount, or there is no dental school near you, check with your local county health department. Many offer low-cost dental services.

LIFE INSURANCE

Life insurance is one of those necessary evils that we'd probably rather not think about. But we need it if we are going to provide for loved ones after the breadwinner dies. Some people may not need much life insurance. Young people will most likely have no one to provide for, but may want a minimal policy to cover funeral expenses and outstanding debts. People without dependents or whose children are grown and independent, or those leaving no debts to their survivors, could do with little or no life insurance.

I know of several families that carry no life insurance. Most of these people are barely able to provide for the family with what they bring home. This is a hard call to make, but I hope they are considering the financial devastation that may follow the husband's or wife's death without insurance. Some expect Social Security to take care of their needs. This is not a good idea, since the future stability of that institution is in question, and the amount that Social Security pays is barely enough to pay the rent. Many families somehow come up with the money for cable TV, toys for the kids, or theater tickets but cannot seem to afford insurance. Most families can get a decent policy for the cost of dinner out.

There are two main types of life insurance: term life and cash value. Following is a brief description along with some pros and cons of each type.

AND THE WINNER IS . . .

The lowest rates available usually go to someone who falls into all of these categories:

- nonsmoker for the past four years
- normal blood pressure without medication
- no serious illnesses
- not overweight (according to the insurance charts)
- low cholesterol
- no deaths in the immediate family from heart disease before age sixty

---

Term Life Insurance

A term policy provides the face value of the benefit and no more. Premiums are lower in the younger years and increase as you age. Consumer groups recommend this type of policy.

There are different types of term life insurance. Mortgage insurance is a type of term life insurance, called decreasing term life insurance. The premium remains the same, but its value shrinks over time as the mortgage balance shrinks.

Cash Value Life Insurance

These policies accrue interest over the life of the policy. They have a variety of names: annuity plans, endowment plans, variable life insurance, traditional whole life, single-premium whole life, interest-sensitive whole life, and universal life insurance.

Cash value policies cost more than term policies because they are both life insurance coverage as well as an investment. This is the type of policy that most insurance agents recommend; however, most consumer groups do not offer it because they feel you can invest money with more return and fewer fees elsewhere.

How Much to Buy

The key to providing for your family is to assess their needs. How long do you want them to live as they are currently living without having to rely on a new source of income? That could mean allowing for your spouse to not return to work for an extended period of time. Or perhaps the spouse does not currently work. Then you would want to provide for your current income for a period of time.

The period of time needs to be decided upon by the couple. How long do they want that current level of income? Some financial counselors recommend between five and ten years worth of expenses.

Other factors to take into consideration are any outstanding debts that would be left to the family, any business loans, taxes that

---

LIFE INSURANCE NEEDS TO
CONSIDER COVERING:

Gross Annual Income
Taxes Paid Annually
Future Special Expenses:
   mortgage balance
   business debts
   taxes (sale of business)
   college tuition
   funeral expenses
   medical bills
   state taxes
Any Assets
   real estate, savings, 401k

---

would be due on the sale of a business, medical bills, estate taxes, moving costs if applicable, college tuition for the children, and mortgages.

To calculate the amount you will need, take your current annual salary and deduct any taxes being paid. Multiply this

---

WAYS TO SAVE

For the best savings, sometimes up to 50 percent over outside agencies, take advantage of any group policies you may be eligible for. Look for them in your workplace, clubs, spouse's clubs or service groups, universities, fraternities, unions, and military organizations. Many employers offer two times the employee's annual salary as a free benefit and then allow the purchase of subsequent coverage at a low fee. This will be your best deal.

To the insurance company we are a statistic: a group type, a risk category, and an age bracket. These are what will determine our costs for coverage. But not all companies consider the same statistic to be at the same level of risk. For example, one company may consider the area where you live as more risky than another company does. So shop around.

Stop smoking. Many insurers charge double to insure a smoker.

Make sure that your weight falls into their desired category. It may pay to lose a few pounds.

Consider mail-order insurance providers. Their premiums can be up to 20 percent lower because they have no insurance agent's commission to pay.

Another way to save as much as 35 percent is to purchase a policy with your spouse. This type is called a first-to-die policy, and it pays just like it sounds. This is cheaper than two individual policies.

Avoid special travel insurance that is sold in airports. Travel is usually covered by general life insurance policies.

---

amount by the number of years you want to provide for. Then add in any extra expenses that may be needed in the future, as listed above. This will be the benefit amount that you should obtain a policy for.

Coverage You Didn't Know You Had

Many of us are covered for life insurance through credit card companies and jobs. The amount of the policy may not be much, but it is worth investigating. Many credit cards automatically cover you for $5,000 of life insurance, and many employers cover their employees if they are killed while working (such as during travel on a business trip). This is in addition to the policies you purchased through the same employer.

--------------------------  --------------------------

Healthcare for Less: Getting the Care You Need—Without Breaking the Bank, Michelle Katz (Hatherleigh, 2006).

The Savvy Patient: How to Get the Best Health Care (Capital Cares), Mark Pettus (Capital Books, 2007).

Stay Well Without Going Broke: Winning the War Over Medical Bills, Pattie Vargas (Unknown, 1994).

Winning the Insurance Game, Ralph Nader (Doubleday, 1993).

CHAPTER 28

Utilities

Our utility bill was another item in our budget that, like groceries, fluctuated. That meant we could make some changes and perhaps save money. With some research and a few simple changes, we were able to reduce our overall utility bill by 25 percent.

First, we had a free energy audit on our home by our local utility company. (Some areas charge a fee for this service.) They reviewed our usage patterns over the past year and made recommendations for energy savings.

WHERE HEAT ESCAPES

33% Floors, ceilings, walls
15% Air ducts
14% Fireplace
13% Pipes (plumbing)
11% Doors
10% Windows
 2% Fans and vents
 2% Electrical outlets

The most enlightening information was how much energy each appliance was costing. This determined the order that I was going to work on our energy expenses. Following is a chart that shows the energy use of the most common household appliances. I based the cost on the kilowatts per hour that each uses and the energy rate for our area. It is meant as a general guideline for your expenses.

For a more accurate determination of the costs you are incurring, have your local utility company explain your rates or perform an energy audit.

Energy Use Chart	
Appliance	**Estimated % of Your Utility Bill**
Lighting the house NOTE: One light bulb costs only 1 to 2 pennies per hour so don't fight over turning a light on and off. It's the many lights over many hours that add up.	9%
Vampire power: Keeping appliances powered on even when not in use	5%
Washing machine (cold vs. hot wash)	5% to 10%
Water heater Note: Insulate the water heater and reduce this number	10%
Refrigerator	15%
Freezer (separate from refrigerator)	5%
Clothes dryer	6%
Central air-conditioner	15%
Gas furnace Space heaters (add an additional 10%)	15%
Dishwasher	2%
Oven (gas vs. electric)	5% to 10%
Computer/television These draw as little as a light bulb and don't add up to much unless many units are left on for hours and hours.	3%

COST-SAVING MEASURES

Here are some changes that can be easily implemented in most homes.

Water Heater

Turning down the temperature of your water heater saves more than you think. For every ten degrees that you turn the heater down, you can save 6 to 10 percent of its energy costs. Most energy advisers recommend that you not turn the temperature below 120 degrees because many automatic dishwashers require a minimum temperature of 120 degrees in order to function properly. Check your dishwashing manual for specific requirements.

Many people wash their dishes by hand in order to save hot water. Depending on how you hand-wash your dishes, it may cost you more to wash by hand. If you run the water for each dish to be rinsed, you may be using more hot water than an automatic dishwasher. For maximum savings, fill one basin for washing and one basin for rinsing and turn the water off.

The water heater's location is key to its best performance. If it is far from the appliances that use it most (like in a garage), much of the energy is wasted as the water travels through the pipes. You can waste 10 to 15 percent of the energy used to heat the water by having it travel. If moving the water heater is too costly, insulate the pipes that carry the water to the appliances.

For other ways to reduce the costs of your water heater, try these:

- Wrap the heater in a special insulating blanket.
- If you have an electric water heater, install an appliance timer that turns it down during nonuse hours (like sleeping hours and vacations).

- Reduce the use of hot water where you can—showering accounts for 30 percent of hot water use in most homes; laundry accounts for 14 percent.

- Don't use the rinse/hold function on your dishwasher. Rinse them yourself, in cold water.

- If you need to replace the water heater, make sure the new one has a high energy-efficiency rating. Even if other water heaters are cheaper, the higher energy-efficiency rating will pay off. Consider a tankless system, which saves even more.

- By washing and rinsing clothes in cold water instead of hot, you can save over $150 per year.

Water

Since fresh water is only a small percentage of the water available on this planet, we need to use it wisely. Saving money is another good motivator. I have lived through three drought periods and can never go back to wasting water the way I used to. Many of us don't realize how much we are using.

Outdoors, much of the groundwater is lost to evaporation, so we put mulch around the plants and trees to trap the moisture in the ground, and we timed sprinklers to go on at night so that little was lost to heat. We replaced our kids' sprinkler games with squirt-gun games. We wash the car with a nozzle that shuts off between uses. We don't wash the patio if we can sweep it instead.

Indoors, we try to double up on baths for the littlest kids. They don't get too dirty and can either share a bath or use the tub one after the other. We wash clothes only when they need it. Some folks find it easier to throw clothes in the hamper than to hang them up at the end of the day.

If you don't have a low-flow toilet, you can create one. Fill a two-liter plastic jug (soda bottle) with water and sink it in the toilet tank. This will reduce the amount of water used with each flush.

We like baths but know that showers save on water usage. A typical shower uses four times less water than a bath. And a low-flow showerhead can save you another 40 percent on water usage. A tub with less water will be as thrifty as a shower. A long shower probably costs as much as a full tub.

The dishwasher uses 10 to 15 gallons of water per washing, so only run it when needed and when full. The dishwasher still uses less water than doing dishes by hand, since most of us let the water run to rinse dishes. Don't use the rinse/hold function when you can rinse them yourself before loading.

Here are some more ideas for water savings:

- When taking a shower, wet yourself, turn the water off, wash, then turn the water on to rinse.
- Don't let the water run while brushing teeth or shaving.
- Fix any leaking faucets and running toilets. These can lead up to dozens of gallons wasted per day.
- Install aerators on all faucets.
- Don't use running water to thaw frozen meat. Let meat sit in cold water instead, or thaw in the refrigerator.
- Run the dishwasher with full loads only.

Laundry

Most of the expenses of doing laundry come from creating heat—the heat of the water and the heat of the dryer. You can reduce the washing machine's energy usage by 90 percent by washing and rinsing in cold water only. The average cost of washing and drying a load of laundry is about a dollar per load. That is based on a cold-water wash and an electric dryer. Of course rates might vary with your utility company.

To maximize the savings with your laundry, try these ideas:

- Always wash a full load. The cost of washing two medium loads is more than one full load.

- Always dry a full load, but don't overfill the dryer; air needs to circulate between the clothes.

- Line dry whenever you can. Purchase a drying rack for indoor drying in the winter. Or stretch a couple of lines across the laundry room. To soften towels, run them in the dryer for a few minutes, then line dry.

- As mentioned above, wash and rinse in cold water and save over $150 per year.

- To cut down on ironing the more casual clothes, spray the clean, dry clothes with diluted fabric softener (¼ cup softener to 2 cups water), smooth with your hands, and hang on a hanger.

- Dry similar fabrics together so the dryer will quit sooner. One towel in a load of permanent-press clothes will keep the whole load running longer.

- Dry loads of clothes one after the other, capturing the heat already in the dryer.

- Make sure the dryer vent is straight. A bent one will reduce airflow and dryer efficiency.

- Clean the lint trap after every load. Lint reduces airflow, and the dryer has to work harder to do the job.

- Check with your utility company for discounts on energy during off-peak hours. Only run the appliances during those hours to save even more.

Heating and Cooling

To efficiently heat a house, you must stop air from leaking in where it isn't welcome. Air leaks are one of the major wastes of energy. They usually cost you another 10 percent in energy costs. I found them around our doors and windows and in my fireplace damper. Anywhere two sections meet in a house (a wall and a window, a wall and a door, a vent and a ceiling) is a good place to check for an air leak. There are several easy ways to tell if there is a leak. The quickest way is to light a candle and slowly move it around the edges of the opening. If it flickers, there is an air leak. (Please be careful not to set the curtains on fire as you do this!) For a safer way, have someone blow air with a hair dryer around edges while you stand outside feeling for the air.

Once I found where my leaks were, I sealed them up with felt weather stripping, found at most hardware stores. For some joints I used caulking. This is especially helpful outside for sealing around the joints between the walls and foundation, or the meeting of the brick and walls. For the fireplace, there are foam blocks you can buy to put in the damper door to seal any cracks. Check for fire hazards before using caulk or any permanent materials in the fireplace. The whole weatherizing treatment cost fifteen dollars. My central heater used to go on four times per night, but now it only goes on one time per night.

> Save $1,200 per year by turning the house furnace down to 50 degrees and heating only the rooms you sleep in with energy-efficient room heaters.

Other ideas for reducing heating costs:

- Change or clean your furnace filter every month it is used. Dust gathers and makes the furnace work harder. This will save you 15 percent of your heating costs.

- Plant trees for sun and wind protection. Get a tree that sheds leaves (deciduous) in the winter so it blocks sun on the house in the summer and lets the sun shine on the house in the winter. This could save you 10 to 30 percent in heating and cooling costs.

- Insulate your attic and walls to the highest R-value that your county building code recommends. This will reduce your heating costs by 20 to 30 percent.

- Close the damper on your fireplace after the ashes are cold. This could reduce your heating loss by 10 percent.

- Check if there is a draft or excessive heat (such as a fireplace) near the thermostat in the house. It may be kicking the furnace or air-conditioner on when the rest of the house is fine.

- Turn the thermostat down (in the winter) and wear more warm clothing. For every degree that you lower the thermostat, you save 3 percent on energy costs. (Use caution when turning down the heat if you are ill or elderly. It may not be medically advised, or in the case of the elderly, some can easily suffer hypothermia with minor temperature reduction.)

- Close off the vent and shut doors to rooms not being used.

- If you are moving to a new home, consider a bi-level house instead of a long ranch-style house. Heat escapes through the roof, so the more roof surface you have, the more heat loss you will have.

- Consider an attic fan to suck the hot air out and circulate air in the house. These drop the temperature in a house by at least ten degrees with little energy usage. In the winter they can keep heating bills lower as well.

- Avoid using a wood fireplace for heating; 90 percent of the heat that a fire generates goes up the chimney. Fireplaces also tend to suck the warm air out of the house. Install glass doors over the fireplace that will allow heat in but will not take heat out with the fire. Or invest in a stove or fireplace insert that uses and distributes heat efficiently.

- If wood is plentiful and cheap in your area, and you have a fireplace stove, wood may be a cheaper source of heating than electricity or gas.

The Kitchen

The first thing I did to conserve energy in my kitchen was to get rid of the extra freezer I had. It wasn't actually in my kitchen (it was in the garage), but I considered it an extension of my kitchen, as it held all my extra food. When the energy audit revealed that it was responsible for 15 to 20 percent of my utility bill, I questioned its cost effectiveness. I figured it was costing twenty dollars per month to run. At that time, that was 20 percent of our utility bill. I was buying in bulk and storing food in there, but the savings on bulk foods was being spent on the appliance to store them in. This seemed illogical. At that particular time we needed every dollar we could save, and twenty dollars could help pay off another bill or pay for four or five meals.

I was determined to find a way to do without it. I made more frequent trips to the day-old bread store (or other outlets for special bulk purchases) instead of once a month. This way I didn't need to store as much food. I learned to freeze meals in plastic bags and lay them flat so the foods took up less room in the freezer. As I've said, the wire rack I purchased created a shelf in my refrigerator freezer, giving me more storage space. Once I was confident I could do without it, I sold the freezer.

When I cook, I can easily conserve energy with some minor changes. When I bake, I try to bake several things at once so the oven is not heated for just one dish. For smaller dishes, the microwave or toaster oven is more energy efficient. I don't preheat the oven unless I am baking breads. I try not to peek at the foods while cooking, since I will lose as much as 20 percent of the heat trapped in there. If you have a self-cleaning oven, clean it right after you are finished baking. You are then using the heat already trapped in the oven. For maximum air circulation, make sure the racks in the oven are not covered with foil. Any blockage of the air movement means the oven will heat unevenly and give false temperature readings.

For range-top cooking, the pan should match the burner size. A small pan on a large burner will waste 40 percent of the heat generated. By using a lid on all pans, you can use three times less energy to cook a dish. Copper-bottomed pans heat up faster and require less energy to cook foods.

Other ideas for saving energy in the kitchen:

- If you have a choice between gas and electric ranges and ovens, the gas version will save you money. Do not consider remodeling for that reason, though, without having a professional compare the savings you will gain over the cost of the remodeling.

- A gas range/oven with an automatic ignition saves 40 to 50 percent more than a pilot light.

- Turn off the range or oven a few minutes before the food is done. Heat still remains on the burner or in the oven.

- Boil water on the range, not in the microwave oven. The microwave uses more energy to do the job, and they take about the same amount of time.

- Broiling is more energy efficient than baking.

- Check with your utility company for discounts on energy during off-peak hours. Only run the oven during those hours to save even more.

- In the summer, do your baking and dishwashing in the evening to avoid heating up the house. In the winter, do these activities in the morning (to help heat up the house).

Lighting

Most light bulbs are incandescent. These are inefficient makers of light. They use 10 percent of their energy for producing light, while 90 percent is wasted on the heat they produce. Fluorescent bulbs use 65 to 75 percent less energy to produce light, and they last ten times longer than incandescent bulbs. The Energy Use Chart earlier in this chapter can be deceptive when we talk about lighting costs. It says that we spend only one cent per hour on light bulbs that are turned on, but we tend to forget how quickly this adds up. We usually have several bulbs on, and we tend to leave them on for several hours.

Try some of the compact fluorescent bulbs that now fit every type of socket. These can create significant savings. And check with your local utility company to see if they are offering rebates on those bulbs. Try these ideas to reduce some of your lighting costs:

- Clear light bulbs give off more light than frosted versions.

- Many bulbs can be replaced by lower-wattage bulbs and still meet your lighting needs.

- Keep the bulb clean: dust and dirt can decrease the bulb's efficiency and life span.

- When buying bulbs, don't go by the wattage; the lumens determine how much light is produced. Each bulb has a lumen number on it: For a brighter room, pick a higher number of lumens. For soft lighting, pick a lower lumen number.

- A light-colored lampshade will allow more light.

- Only light the area of a room where you are working or reading. The whole room doesn't need to be lit.

- Turn off lights when you leave a room.

- Avoid the long-life bulbs. They cost you more in the long run because they use more energy. Stick with less expensive lower-wattage bulbs.

------------------------- *Resources* -------------------------

The Complete Guide to Reducing Energy Costs, Consumer Reports (Consumer Reports, 2006).

Consumer Guide to Home Energy Savings: Save Money, Save the Earth, 9th Edition, Jennifer Thorne Amann (New Society Publishers, 2007).

CHAPTER 29

Crafts for Kids

There are many days when my kids are asking for something to do. I could buy a craft or some other toy, but I have found my budget doesn't allow for those solutions. It's amazing what a little imagination can do. When I lived in Nigeria and Pakistan, I saw kids make toys out of things they found. They inspired me to be less dependent on ready-made toys. I began researching ways to make our crafts. My kids appreciate the time I have invested. The cost is minimal, and we have fun together. Below are some ideas we have enjoyed.

Kids' Aprons

I don't believe in buying a special apron for kids (unless it's from a garage sale). Aprons are expensive and the kids outgrow them quickly. Instead of a ready-made apron, we turn my husband's old long-sleeved shirts into paint and craft aprons. The kids wear the shirts backward (so the buttons are in the back) with the cuffs rolled up slightly. The shirts are long enough to cover their clothes well.

Bubbles That Last

> 5 C. water
> ½ C. liquid Dawn or Joy
> 2 T. glycerin (at drugstores)

Pour water into container first. Add dish soap and glycerin and stir (try not to make it froth). Dip a bubble wand into the solution and blow!

Bubble wands: For homemade bubble wands, try bending wire into any shape (a coat hanger works). Provide adult supervision because of the sharp ends.

Bird Cookies

> wooden tree ornaments or shapes (¼ inch thick)
> peanut butter
> birdseed
> string

Punch a hole (using a nail and hammer) in the top of the shape and add a string loop. Slather wooden shapes with peanut butter. Roll in birdseed. Hang outside where you can watch the birds eat.

Bird Treats

> ½ C. peanut butter
> ½ C. flour
> 1½ C. birdseed

Mix well and shape into a ball. Press flat to ½ inch thick. Place on baking sheet. Gently poke a hole in the middle of the "cookie." Bake at 425° for 30 minutes. Cool completely. Hang with string outside.

How to Make Paper

This is not only a craft but also a lesson in recycling.

- several pieces of paper (newspaper, notebook paper, or even paper bags)
- bucket or other container to soak the paper
- blender
- magnifying glass
- window screen on a wooden frame (screen can be bought at the hardware store, or art stores sell plain wooden frames to which you can staple screen)
- dry newspaper or felt

Tear the paper into small squares and soak in water for several hours. Place ½ cup of paper in blender. Fill the blender with water from the bucket. Blend the paper for 30 seconds. Blending makes paper pulp. Put some pulp on your finger and look at it under the magnifying glass. There are tiny wood fibers.

Over a sink, spread the layer of pulp evenly onto the screen and drain the water. Place a layer of newspaper on the pulp and press out the rest of the water. Turn the screen over while holding the newspaper on it so the newspaper is on the bottom. Carefully lift off the screen. Gently place another layer of newspaper over the pulp and press the water out again. Turn the newspaper over and repeat the pressing with more dry paper. Repeat several times. Gently peel off the new paper and place on dry paper. Dry overnight.

Fun things to try with your papermaking:

- Add 1 tablespoon of laundry starch: This creates a shinier finish on the paper surface.
- Add decorations such as flowers or leaves to your paper pulp as you pour it onto the screen.

• Add food coloring to the pulp mix for colored paper.

Leaf Painting

Collect leaves of different types and vein patterns. Paint an even coat of nontoxic paint on top of a sponge. Place the ribbed side of the leaf on top of the sponge. Place a piece of paper on the leaf and press gently for ten to fifteen seconds. Place the leaf, paint side down, on a piece of paper. Put another piece of paper on top and rub gently for another ten to fifteen seconds. Remove top paper carefully and gently peel off leaf, holding it by its stem.

Torn Paper Art

Save single sheets of colored paper or construction paper that aren't being used. I save flyers that are printed on one side of colored paper. Tear them into small pieces (¼-inch each). Draw a basic outline on a sheet of white paper of what you want to make (such as a Christmas tree, a wreath, a boat, etc.), and glue the torn pieces of paper into the design.

We made a Christmas tree by drawing a triangle for the tree and filling it in with torn green pieces, then adding a few red and blue pieces for ornaments, and a few brown pieces (from a brown paper bag) for the trunk.

Modeling Dough

Kids can help mix this. Add more fun by using rolling pins, potato mashers, and cookie cutters.

1½ C. flour
½ C. salt
food coloring (optional)
½ C. water
¼ C. vegetable oil

In a bowl, mix flour and salt together. To the water, add food coloring, 2 or 3 drops at a time (until desired color is reached), and stir. Slowly add colored water and oil to dough and mix well. Knead dough by hand until soft.

Note: Sprinkle with a little flour and knead in if dough is too sticky. Leftover dough can be stored in plastic bags or airtight containers to keep it soft.

Play Dough

This is like the above recipe but has a slightly different texture and lasts longer.

2 C. flour
1 C. salt
4 tsp. cream of tartar
2 C. water with food coloring
2 T. oil

Mix all ingredients together in a pan (nonstick is better). Cook over medium heat, stirring constantly, until it forms a hard ball.

As it becomes half cooked, the dough is hard to mix. Keep stirring until all parts are hardened. Remove from the pan and knead to achieve a smooth consistency. This batch of play dough will cost only thirty cents as compared to between two and three dollars for store-bought.

Note: For glitter dough, add glitter when cooking is finished and you are kneading dough.

Try using unsweetened drink mix for the coloring. It also adds fragrance. Use one pack for each recipe.

Edible Modeling Clay

1 C. peanut butter
1 C. nonfat dry milk

$^1\!/_3$ C. powdered sugar
1 C. loose coconut (optional)

Place peanut butter in a large bowl and work in dry milk with fingers. Add powdered sugar and coconut and work in with fingers. The texture should be like play dough. If it's too dry, add more peanut butter. If it's too sticky, add more dry milk. This keeps well in a plastic bag for a week. Try making spiders by rolling a ball for the tummy and one for the head. Use pretzel sticks for the legs and raisins for the eyes.

3-D Salt Map Dough

This is a versatile medium for many projects such as relief maps for school, Christmas ornaments, homemade buttons, and other crafts.

3 C. salt
3 C. flour
2 C. water (approximate)
Poster board, foam board, or thin plywood

Mix salt and flour thoroughly and set aside. Heat the water to boiling, and add enough to the salt and flour mixture to reach the consistency of frosting. Keep in mind that the more water you use, the longer the dough will take to dry. Draw a picture of what you want to make on a board. Spread the mixture within the boundaries, piling it up to make a three-dimensional pattern. After the dough dries (one to three days), paint with poster paints.

Aromatic Modeling Dough

This is fun to make at Christmastime. One woman makes it into a piecrust with the top layer latticed and puts potpourri inside the "pie." Another made ornaments with it by rolling the dough, cutting out shapes, piercing a hole for string or ribbon, and drying them.

¾ C. applesauce
1 C. cinnamon (4 oz.)
1 T. cloves
1 T. nutmeg
2 T. glue

Mix all ingredients thoroughly and shape into figures (snowmen, bowls, etc.). Lay on cookie sheet and leave in oven overnight with only the oven light on (or at 150° for a few hours).

Painted Pebbles

Gather stones outdoors, looking for unusual shapes and sizes. Paint with acrylic paint or watercolors. Glue on wobbly eyes to make faces. For a fine finish, apply a coat of clear nail polish when the paint is dry. These make fun gifts for grandparents.

Make a family by hot-gluing several "people" to a piece of driftwood.

Rock Candy

This is fun and teaches patience too.

1 C. water
3½ C. sugar
heat-resistant glass jar
3 10-in. lengths of clean string
pencil

Boil the water in a saucepan. Start adding the sugar a couple of tablespoons at a time. Stir as the sugar dissolves and syrup forms. Keep an eye on the pan at all times so the syrup doesn't boil over. When all the sugar is dissolved and the syrup is clear, remove from the heat and let cool for ten minutes. Pour into glass jar.

Tie one end of each of the lengths of string to the pencil, leaving a space between each one. Rest the pencil over the jar, with the strings lowered into the syrup.

Check the jar daily, but do not disturb. The crystals will form on the strings in about two weeks. If crystals form over the surface, break them up carefully so further evaporation will continue. The candy is "done" whenever you have the amount of crystals you desire. The longer you leave it, the more crystals there will be and the larger they will grow.

Fireworks in January

Color a piece of paper with red, blue, and green crayons (color in large patches of each color). Cover all of the paper. Paint over it with black poster paint or ink. Let it dry. Scratch off firework shapes with a toothpick.

Street Chalk

> 1 C. plaster of Paris (do not pack)
> almost ½ C. cool water
> 2 to 3 T. liquid acrylic paint
> small paper cups

Pour plaster into a disposable container. Using a disposable stirring stick, stir in most of the water. Add paint and mix well. Add a little more water as the mixture thickens. Stir well and pour into paper cups. Peel off the paper when the chalk is dry.

Juice Lids

Ever wonder what to do with those concentrated juice can lids (the round metal discs with smooth edges)? Here are a few ideas:

- Make refrigerator magnets by gluing small magnets (available by the pack at most craft stores) on the backs and decorating the fronts with the following ideas:

  - Paint with different colors of fabric glue.

  - Paint on a thin layer of white glue and cover with sand. Shake off excess. When dry, paste on a cutout camel or other desert animal, or small shells.

  - Glue on a favorite wallet-sized photo (cut to the size and shape of the lid).

  - Create sorting toys for younger children. Save any container that has a lid (oatmeal box, large yogurt container, etc.) and cut a slit in the lid. Let the little ones put the juice lids in the box one at a time.

Goop

This is much like Gak, found in toy stores, but this recipe will not stain everything it touches, and it washes out of fabrics (unlike the store-bought version). It also makes a great science project because it is the result of a chemical reaction. The homemade version costs about $1.75.

> 8 oz. Elmer's glue (use school glue, not Glue-All or washable glue)
> ¾ C. water, plus food coloring
> 1 tsp. 20 Mule Team Borax (in laundry aisles of most grocery stores)
> ½ C. water

In a large bowl, combine the first 2 ingredients until well blended. In a separate cup, combine the Borax and water until the Borax is dissolved. Pour the Borax solution into the glue solution and stir. A large lump will form. Work the lump with your hands. As you work the lump, the glue will be absorbed and the lump will become smooth. Store in an airtight plastic box or zippered plastic bag. It will last a few weeks.

Note: If the Goop gets on clothing or fabric, try to wash it before it dries. Spraying with a pretreatment helps. If the Goop dries and hardens before you notice, soak the area overnight, scraping off as much as possible, and then wash in warm water.

Creepy Slime

> 1 C. cornstarch
> ½ C. cold water
> green food coloring (or other color)

Mix all ingredients in a bowl. Put it in your hand and it slowly creeps. Pound on it on the table and it's solid. Which is it?

Silly Putty

> ¼ C. liquid laundry starch
> ¼ C. Elmer's school glue

Mix together. Some have found that mixing inside a plastic bag works best. Store in a plastic container or in the refrigerator. This makes enough for a few kids to each have a glob.

Finger Paint

> 2 T. cool water
> 2 T. cornstarch
> 1 C. boiling water
> food coloring

Mix the cool water and cornstarch. Add the boiling water and

stir. It should thicken as you stir. When it is cool, divide into small cups or muffin tins. Then add food coloring and mix.

Note: To remove any stains these create, try the stain-removal ideas in the next chapter, "Safer and Cheaper Cleaning Supplies."

Quick and Cheap Finger Paint

Mix a few drops of food coloring with some inexpensive shaving cream. The kids can color on paper that is spread on the kitchen table or decorate the bathtub tile. The latter is an easier place to clean up.

MOO-ving Milk

½ C. whole milk
few drops food coloring
few drops liquid detergent

Pour milk into a pie plate or bowl. Drop some food coloring into the milk but don't let the drops touch each other. Add a few drops of detergent and watch the colors swirl. Why is this happening? The detergent is causing the milk fat to separate.

Resources

Crafting Fun: 101 Things to Make and Do with Kids, Rae Grant (St. Martin's Griffin, 2008).

Creative Crafts for Kids, Gill Dickerson and Cheryl Owen (Hamlyn, 2005).

CHAPTER 30

Safer and Cheaper Cleaning Supplies

Store shelves are filled with products we are told we "need" to use in order to effectively clean our homes. Most of them do a great job. But at what price? It's important to note that they aren't necessary in order to do a good job of cleaning. I found my great-grandmother's notebook of homemade cleaning recipes. It was inspiring to find alternatives to ready-made cleaning products.

Aside from my interest in being frugal, I began to research alternative cleaners to combat my son's chemical sensitivity. The more I use them, the happier I am at the effect on my pocketbook, my kids, and the environment.

We don't need special cleaning products for each cleaning need. We don't need a special bottle for tile cleaning, one for the toilet, and another for countertops, floors, or walls. The cleaning supply manufacturers want you to think you need these—and they make more money. Many of these products are made from the same ingredients.

There are many good books in the library filled with recipes for cleaners. The following are some of the best recipes

I have found—including some from my great-grandmother's notebook.

ALTERNATIVE CLEANING SUPPLIES

Natural cleaners are cheaper. But even though they are natural, they can still cause skin damage. So please wear gloves while cleaning with these substances.

With some basic supplies you can do most of your cleaning. Here is a list of the basic supplies I use and a description of their purpose:

Vinegar

This inexpensive ingredient kills bacteria and mold and can be used as a disinfectant, but without the risk associated with ammonia. Use the distilled type for a less offensive odor. This also can be used to remove soap scum or wash windows, and added to dishwater to make glass sparkle. It can also be used as a stain remover. It has many first-aid uses, such as for beestings, hives, sunburn, sore throats, and upset stomachs. The chemical name for vinegar is acetic acid.

Baking Soda

This is a versatile, nontoxic cleaner also known as sodium bicarbonate. It can be a nonscratch powder for scrubbing metal and tile surfaces. Diluted in water, it deodorizes and cleans refrigerators, stovetops, etc. Sprinkle on carpets to remove odors. Sprinkle on a grease fire to put out the flame. There are literally hundreds of uses for baking soda.

Borax

This is a natural compound also known as sodium borate. It is a cleaner and a water softener. It can be used to scrub metal and tile surfaces without scratching. It can be poured into drains to keep them clean. It cleans floors well too. It is great for neutralizing the ammonia in urine when soaking diapers. It even kills fleas.

Washing Soda

This is a natural compound that is very versatile. It is also called sodium carbonate (not sodium *bi*carbonate). It can be used to freshen laundry and boost laundry detergent. It can also be used to clean bathroom surfaces, greasy stoves, ovens, and grills.

Citrus Peels

Citrus is a fragrant cleaning source. The fruit can be ground up in garbage disposals to freshen and clear out the gunk built up in there. The peels can be boiled and the solution used for cleaning greasy messes, not to mention freshening the air. A manufacturer has bottled this idea in an all-natural solvent called Citra Solv.

THE ENVIRONMENTAL COST OF STORE-BOUGHT: CLEANERS AND CLEANING TOOLS

The first cost is to people. The chemicals in these cleaners are diluted forms of caustic and dangerous elements. They are washed down the drain. Water treatment plants do not remove chemicals. The effect on us is not entirely known at this time.

The second cost is financial. Most cleaners can be replaced with common household items. These common ingredients cost pennies compared to the dollars the cleaners cost.

The third cost is to the environment. We flush these chemicals down the drain and into the water supply, affecting nearby lakes, rivers, plant life, and animals. Municipal water treatment plants don't filter out these chemicals.

Cleaning Tools

Instead of spending money for scrubbing tools, see what you can reuse around the house. For example, when a toothbrush begins to fray and would normally be discarded, I put it with my cleaning supplies. I use it for cleaning grout and tight spots around faucets. It also cleans jewelry with gemstones very well.

CLEANING RECIPES

Following are my favorite cleaning solutions, which are also simple to make.

Furniture Polish

1 part lemon juice
2 parts vegetable or olive oil

Brass Polish

Apply ketchup or Worcestershire sauce. Let stand a few minutes, then rinse. If an area doesn't clean, there must be a buildup of grease or dirt. Clean the residue off with a paste of salt and vinegar, and then reapply the sauce. Or try the natural product Citra Solv, which is made from citrus peels.

Copper Polish

Coat the surface with ketchup. Let it sit for a few minutes, then rinse off. Rub with a soft cloth to dry.

Silver Polish

Make a paste with ¼ cup baking soda and 1½ T. water. Apply with a damp sponge. Rub, then rinse and buff dry. Or put the baking soda in enough boiling water to cover the silverware. Let sit ten minutes, then polish.

Drain Cleaner

¼ C. baking soda
½ C. vinegar

Pour baking soda in drain. Pour vinegar in drain. Tightly close the drain. Let rest a few minutes. Then flush with boiling water. Repeat until clear. To keep the drain free of buildup, weekly flush with ¼ cup salt, then boiling water.

Hard-Water Buildup

Put equal parts vinegar and water inside a teakettle or vase that has mineral buildup. Let sit for at least a half hour. Then scrub out the minerals.

Oven Cleaner

When the spill is still warm, sprinkle with salt and scrub.

Tile and Floor Cleaner

Scrub with a paste of 20 Mule Team Borax and water.

Carpet Cleaner

1 part cornmeal
1 part 20 Mule Team Borax

Combine and sprinkle over carpet. Leave for one hour. Vacuum.

Carpet Odor

Sprinkle baking soda on the carpet and leave overnight. Vacuum well.

Upholstery Cleaner

¼ cup 20 Mule Team Borax
1 T. dishwashing liquid
1 C. warm water

Stir ingredients together. Rub surface with a soft cloth that has been dipped in this solution.

Wall Cleaner

1 gal. hot water
½ C. borax

My Great-Grandma Maggie's Porcelain Cleaner

Rub porcelain with cream of tartar and a damp, soft rag.

Window Cleaner #1

2 C. water
2 T. ammonia

Window Cleaner #2

1 C. vinegar
2 C. water

This does a great job cleaning windows and mirrors.

Toilet Bowl

Sprinkle with baking soda, then pour in a little vinegar. Scrub with a brush. For tougher stains, make a paste of Borax and lemon juice and let it remain on the stain overnight.

Spot Remover for Clothes

Dissolve ¼ cup Borax in 2 cups of cold water. Sponge on and let dry. Wash garment or fabric as recommended. This solution works on blood, chocolate, coffee, mildew, and mud.

Ink

Wet the fabric with water, then apply a paste of cream of tartar and lemon juice. Let sit for an hour, then wash as directed. You can also try spraying the garment with hair spray just before washing.

"Washable" Color Markers

Rinse the stain in cold water until it runs clear. Then wet the stain with rubbing alcohol. Blot with another cloth until the color is removed. Wash in hottest water allowed for the fabric.

Poster Paints and Watercolors (on Garments)

Apply rubbing alcohol to the stain and blot with another cloth until no more color comes off. Line dry. If the stain remains, soak garment in one quart of warm water, one teaspoon of dishwashing liquid, and one tablespoon of vinegar. Wash in hottest water the fabric can tolerate.

Poster Paint, Finger Paint, and Watercolors (on Carpeting)

First remove as much of the paint as possible by applying a paste of baking soda and water to the stain. When the paste is dry, vacuum the spot. To remove what remains, soak a sponge in rubbing alcohol and blot the stain until no more color comes off on the sponge. (I stand on my sponge to encourage the paint to soak up.) If some stain still remains, blot again with a sponge soaked in ammonia.

Silly Putty on Carpeting or Garments

My mom says that when I left Silly Putty on the carpet, she froze it by applying ice. It became brittle and peeled right off.

Chewing Gum in Hair

Slather peanut butter on the gum. It will dissolve it. Then comb it out. Keep doing this until all gum is removed.

Play Dough on Carpeting

Remove larger pieces while dough is still pliable. Let the rest dry into the carpet overnight. Make a solution of warm water with some dishwashing liquid. Use a stiff brush dipped in the water to work the rest of the dough out.

Lipstick

Rub with shortening (not margarine—this has yellow dye in it) then launder.

PERSONAL CLEANSING AND COMFORT

Bath Time

For a soothing bath, add one cup of dry milk to the bath water. For soft skin, add one cup of baking soda as well.

Toothpaste

> 8 T. baking soda
> 3 T. glycerin (available at drugstores)
> 1 to 2 tsp. flavoring (peppermint, orange, etc.)

Blend well and store in an airtight container. For a simpler and quick paste: Mix equal parts baking soda and salt. For flavor, add a dash of cinnamon, mint extract, or flavored fluoride liquid.

Cleansing Cream

> 3 T. coconut oil
> 1 T. vegetable oil
> 1 T. glycerin (available at drugstores)
> 2 tsp. water

Melt these on low heat. Remove from heat and beat with a whisk or fork until well blended. Store in an airtight jar. If your house becomes very hot, keep the cream in the refrigerator.

Astringent

Below are three ways to make astringent. My favorite is the first. It is very refreshing.

- Mix equal parts witch hazel and water, or
- Mix equal parts distilled white vinegar and water, or

- Mash some strawberries—rub them on your face. Rinse with warm water.

Beestings/Sunburn/Hives

Vinegar can instantly relieve the pain and itch of beestings, hives, or sunburn—much faster than a baking soda paste. Soak brown paper (from a paper bag) with vinegar and apply to the affected area.

Antacid

> ½ tsp. baking soda
> ½ C. water

For an upset stomach, combine and drink.

Cuts and Burns

Thoroughly clean an injury—and keep it clean—and you should fare well. Avoid remedies such as iodine, hydrogen peroxide, Merthiolate, Mercurochrome, Bactine, or Campho-Phenique. These damage the skin and can lead to worse scarring.

Ice Bag

> 2 quart-sized resealable plastic bags
> 1 C. water
> ½ C. rubbing alcohol

Put liquid in one bag and seal tightly. Put the other bag around it and seal it for double protection. Freeze. It will be slushy, so it can mold to the wound or swollen area. Place on the skin for ten to twenty minutes.

Note: Wrap with a cloth if skin is sensitive to the cold. Beware of causing frostbite to the area.

My Great-Grandma Maggie's Remedy for Arthritis Pain

Mix rubbing alcohol with a few drops of wintergreen and rub on the affected parts.

Athlete's Foot

> ½ C. apple cider vinegar
> 2 C. hot water

Soak your feet in the solution until it cools. Do this once a day for about a week. It should kill the fungi.

Skin Irritations

For relief of minor burns, itches from insect bites, sunburn, and poison oak or ivy, smooth on the fresh juice of the aloe plant. Keep a plant in the house and break off a leaf, releasing the juices inside. Apply directly to the affected area as often as needed.

Yeast Infections

The live yogurt culture acidophilus, when eaten, is helpful in combating yeast infection.

MISCELLANEOUS REMEDIES

My Great-Grandma Maggie's Remedy for No-Run Stockings

Soak stockings in a mixture of alum (used to make pickles) and water to prevent running.

Garden Pesticide #1

1 T. dishwashing detergent
1 C. vegetable oil

Mix and store in an airtight container. When needed, mix 1 to 2 T. of this solution with 1 C. water. Spray on plants, covering all leaf and stem surfaces. (From the U.S. Department of Agriculture.)

Garden Pesticide #2

3 onions
2 quarts water
4 cloves garlic

Boil these together for an hour. Discard onions and garlic. When liquid is cool, pour into a spray bottle and spray on plants.

Snail Bait

2 tsp. sugar
½ tsp. yeast
2 C. water

Mix in a shallow dish or pie pan. Snails are attracted to this bait and will drown in it.

Weeds

To kill unwanted growth in your garden, pour boiling water directly on weeds. To save plants around the weeds, water good plants and surrounding soil well just before applying the hot water. This cools the plants, and if any hot water seeps onto the good plants, the water already in the soil will cool it down. Make sure you pour the hot water only on the weed.

Resources

Better Basics for the Home: Simple Solutions for Less-Toxic Living, Annie Berthold-Bond (Three Rivers Press, 1999).

Bug Busters: Poison-Free Pest Controls for Your House & Garden, Bernice Lifton (Avery Publishing, 1991).

Clean House, Clean Planet: Clean Your House for Pennies a Day, the Safe, Nontoxic Way, Karen N. Logan (Pocket Books, 1997).

Clean Your House Safely and Effectively Without Harmful Chemicals, Randy Dunford (Magni Company, 1993).

Creating a Healthy Household: The Ultimate Guide for Healthier, Safer, Less-Toxic Living, Lynn M. Bower (Healthy House Institute, 2000).

The Green Kitchen Handbook: Practical Advice, References, and Sources for Transforming the Center of Your Home Into a Healthy, Livable Place, Annie Berthold-Bond (HarperCollins, 1997).

Home Safe Home: Protecting Yourself and Your Family From Everyday Toxins and Harmful Household Products in the Home, Debra L. Dadd (Jeremy P. Tarcher, 1997).

The Naturally Clean Home: 100 Safe and Easy Herbal Formulas for Non-Toxic Cleansers, Karyn Siegel-Maier (Storey Publishing, 1999).

CHAPTER 31

An Easy $10,000: Various Ways to Pocket Some Money

It is amazing how a few small changes can add up to large savings. Each idea here can save you some money. The more ideas you adopt, the more money you will save. If you applied all of these ideas, they could add up to more than an annual savings of $10,000. (This assumes you haven't already been applying any of them.) Your savings may vary from the potential monthly savings listed.

ELECTRICITY

$100   Enroll in load management programs and off-hour-rate programs offered by your utility company.

$100   Turn your furnace down by three degrees (lowering one degree saves up to 3 percent).

$30   Lower the temperature on your hot water heater to between 110 and 120 degrees. It's not necessary to have it any hotter and it wastes energy.

$20   Run your dishwasher only when you have a full load.

$20   Let the dishes air-dry instead of using the heat cycle.

$20   Wash your laundry in cold water.

LONG-DISTANCE SERVICE

$60   Switch to a no-fee service.

$100   Use your cell phone, and make sure you use the cheapest times to call.

$100   Call during off-peak hours.

$100   Use e-mail instead of telephoning.

$100   Use free Internet dialing (e.g., *www.skype.com*).

AUTOMOBILE USE

$100   Keep your engine tuned and your tires inflated to their proper pressure.

$100   Get the junk out of your trunk. The more weight an engine has to pull, the more gas it uses. For every extra 250 pounds your engine hauls, your car consumes an extra mile per gallon of gas.

$200   Fill up the gas tank when near a gas station with low prices.

$100   Turn off the engine if you are idling more than two minutes.

$100   Radial tires are 2% to 3% more fuel efficient.

$100   Watch your speed: a 10-mile-per-hour increase in speed causes a 17 percent decrease in gas mileage.

$100   Check gas prices around town. They can vary by 35 cents per gallon. Visit *www.gasbuddy.com*.

$300   Pay for gas with a gas rebate credit card. Many are offering 5% rebates on gas.

CHECKING ACCOUNT

$100   Choose a checking account with no fees (usually requires a minimum balance).

$50   Have your payroll checks automatically deposited to reduce your monthly bank fees.

$100   Use your own bank's ATM to avoid usage fees.

CREDIT CARDS

$400   Compare annual percentage rates (APR) and switch to a card with a lower rate.

$100   Combine all of the cards you use (gas, department store, etc.) into one or two cards and avoid late-payment and over-the-credit-limit fees.

INSURANCE

$400   Compare rates with other companies in your area.

$100   Reduce or drop comprehensive and/or collision coverage on old cars.

$100   Increase your deductibles.

$100   Get a multi-policy discount by keeping all insurance policies with one company.

$100   Get as many discounts as you can: nonsmoker, low-mileage, antitheft device, good student, senior citizen, military, etc.

BABY CARE

$500   Make your own baby food.

$300   Switch to off-brand diapers.

ENTERTAINMENT

$2,000   Reduce how often you eat out by 50 percent.

$150   Limit movie rentals and use library movies instead.

$600   Don't go to the mall for entertainment. The longer you're there, the more you spend.

$250   Reduce your cable service: eliminate movie channels and step down to minimum service.

$400   If you have movie channels, stop renting movies.

CLOTHES

$700   Plan your clothing needs and buy your clothes at thrift and consignment stores.

VACATIONS

$3,000   Visit friends and relatives instead of amusement parks. Drive instead of fly. Visit local attractions instead of cross-country locales. Take a cooler of food and refill at grocery stores instead of eating out at each meal. Use motels that provide a free meal for kids or where kids stay free.

DECORATING

$1,000   *Curtains*
Buy a good heavy curtain from a thrift store, regardless of the print. Then find a bed sheet in a pattern you like. (Shop sales, thrift stores, or bedding outlets, and buy several.) The curtains I bought were a perfect fit for a full-sized sheet. Some may be the same size as two full-sized sheets sewn together. Wash the curtains in cold water and fluff-dry or line-dry for minimum shrinkage. Take out any bunching or pleating but leave the hems on the edges intact. The curtain should resemble a large rectangle. Sew the sheet around the edges of the curtain to cover the curtain. (A sheet alone would be too sheer.) Reapply any pleats and hang. Hem bottom of curtains after hanging. My six living room curtains cost a total of $55.

Valances

Using a 2' x 4' piece of wood, cut it to the width of your window. Sew fabric of your choice into a tube (twice the length of the board) and ease it onto the board. Fix it to the top of the window trim or nail it to the wall above the window.

Furniture

Garage sales and thrift stores have provided top name-brand sofa and overstuffed chairs that have no wear on them for $150. One family I know builds their own furniture. They find furniture manufacturers or staircase makers and take the scraps of wood left from their projects. Usually the wood is given free of charge as long as they pick it up. My friend's latest project is an armoire entertainment center. It is made of solid oak scraps. The total cost was less than $20 for hinges and supplies.

Sofa Recovering

If you have a fine sofa but the covering has had it from all those little feet and spilled drinks, here is a creative idea. Find some fabric you like. For this you can again use a sheet, or buy a heavier fabric at an upholstery fabric outlet store. They have the ends of fabric rolls used by furniture stores. Remove the old sofa fabric in sections with a razor edge, and use these pieces as the pattern (add two inches to each side for tucking and mistakes). Attach the new fabric to the existing seams with a staple gun. Our love seat cost me $60 to redo myself. I was quoted $500 to have it done by someone else.

SEASONAL SAVINGS

$1,000+ Almost everything we need for our homes goes on
sale at some time during the year.

JANUARY TO FEBRUARY—white sale, Presidents' Day sale
Clothes: men's shirts
Linens: towels, linens, sheets
Appliances: stock clearance, clothes dryers, used cars, water
heaters
Household: weatherizing treatments, art supplies, bicycles,
books, curtains
Furniture: most furniture
Gifts: Christmas wrap and ornaments, toys, etc.
Groceries: meats (turkey, ham), baking items

MARCH—end-of-winter sale, pre-spring sale
Clothes: coats, clothes for all, shoes
Appliances: TVs, housewares, washing machines
Household: ski equipment
Groceries: artichokes

APRIL TO MAY—after-Easter sale, pre-summer sale, Mother's
Day sale, Memorial Day sale
Clothes: dresses, suits, coats, summer clothes
Linens: towels
Appliances: TVs, tires
Household: outdoor furniture, paint, tools, garden supplies,
camping and boating equipment
Gifts: gift items
Groceries: artichokes, dairy products, ham, eggs, chicken

JUNE TO JULY—Father's Day sale, end-of-school sale, after-
July 4 sale
Clothes: summer clothes, shoes

Appliances: air-conditioners
Household: school supplies, outdoor furniture, building materials
Furniture: most furniture
Gifts: gift items
Groceries: dairy products, fresh fish, barbecue foods

AUGUST TO SEPTEMBER—end-of-summer sale, pre-fall sale, Labor Day sale
Clothes: summer clothes, fall clothes, school clothes, swimwear
Household: school supplies, garden supplies and tools, outdoor furniture, rugs and carpets, car batteries and mufflers, bicycles
Groceries: fresh fish, lamb, canned goods

OCTOBER—pre-holiday sales
Household: summer sports equipment, cars from dealerships (buy close to the last day of the month for the best deal)

NOVEMBER—holiday sales, Black Friday
Clothes: men's shirts
Appliances: water heaters
Household: home improvement supplies, homes are cheaper
Groceries: spices (stock up!)

DECEMBER

December is probably the best month for sales.

DAY OF THE WEEK

Seasons aren't the only thing that dictate price. The day of the week you make your purchase also can affect price. Keep these tricks in mind:

Airplane Tickets—buy and fly on *Wednesdays*. The lower fares are posted midweek after the weekend tickets are bought and the airlines start to slash prices to compete for sales. Also, flying on a Tuesday or Wednesday tends to be cheaper than any other day of the week.

Cars—Car dealers do the bulk of their selling on the weekends. If they had a slow weekend, or if it's close to the end of the month, a hungry salesman on a slow *Monday* can be very willing to make you a deal.

Clothing—Most department stores stock their shelves on Thursdays. This is also when they begin their weekend specials. So by *Thursday evening*, you should have good pickings and low prices.

Dinner Out—Most restaurants have slow sales midweek and tend to run specials to encourage you to come in on those nights. *Tuesdays* tend to be the most popular for good deals such as "kids eat free" or "half off the second meal."

Groceries—The sales run from Wednesday through Tuesday or Sunday through Saturday. On the night before the sale ends, the stores are likely to have run out of items that were on special. Why am I telling you to go when they are out? Get a rain check for those items and buy them later when you need them, or when you might have a bit more cash available.

CHAPTER 32

Five Questions I Get Asked Most Often

For years I wrote a column that was published in several newsletters and Web sites called *Ask Miserly Moms*. People wrote in their questions and I would give them an answer. After seventeen years of writing the column and doing interviews, many of the same questions kept being asked. Here are the five most frequently asked questions, along with my answers.

1. **You say that you only spent $40 per week on groceries. What did you eat?**

   When we first embarked on our frugal lifestyle, I heard critics say that they would never want to live frugally since it meant having to eat "frugal food." They didn't believe that anyone could serve healthy food to their family while on a tight budget.

   At the beginning of our frugal adventure, we lived on forty dollars a week for groceries. Since we were living on half of our usual income, we had to cut the grocery bill down this low to pay other bills. Despite this tight budget, we ate plenty of produce and adequate protein, and were even able to cook around my son's restrictive food allergies.

The key to serving healthy frugal meals is to think differently: It isn't about **what** you are cooking but **how** you shopped for it and **who** prepared it. Serving fried potatoes is not the definition of frugal food. I eat what everyone else eats: chicken, vegetables, and grains. I can serve salmon to the family if I buy it on sale. I just can't run out and buy the individually frozen portions at full retail price—that will cost me triple. And if you buy ready-made health food, then you will overspend. So in theory, my neighbor and I can serve the exact same meal, but she will pay fifteen dollars for it and I will pay five dollars.

Cooking healthy has the same guidelines as any other type of shopping that I describe in this book: Plan menus around sales, don't shop at just one store, buy in bulk, and avoid convenience foods.

No one should be able to tell that you live frugally if you do it right. The same recipes can be served, but the ingredients will have cost you less. The only difference might be that you can't arbitrarily plan the menu around what you feel like serving that week, but instead have to work around what's on sale. But unless you told someone why you picked fajitas and beef stew over fried chicken that night, no one would know. With the right approach and attitude, your frugal cooking will be an enhancement to your family's budget, not a frustration.

2. *Prices are about the same everywhere. Does it really make a difference? And what about the cost of driving around, and your time?*

Earlier in the book I went into great detail about how little time it took me to save hundreds of dollars per week. Without repeating the breakdown of the costs, just let me summarize in saying that for only a few hours per week, you can transform your family's budget. If prices were about the same everywhere, then that statement wouldn't be true. Shopping sales would be rather worthless. But that is not true.

When we first embarked on our frugal journey, I thought like everyone else: Prices are about the same everywhere. Once I began researching things, I saw that wasn't true. The marketing companies would like you to think that's true so you will buy their product, but beware of that trap. Once you look at the unit prices (ounce, each, etc.), you can see the difference. When cereal boxes are not uniform in size, ranging from 8 ounces to 42 ounces, it's hard to know which one is the best deal. But once you do the math and compare ounce to ounce, you can easily see the huge swing in prices.

I had a local TV news crew follow me around one day. I went to three stores to get the sale items, and then did the rest of my shopping at a local inexpensive grocery store. I shopped unit price and avoided convenience foods. In the end, I had saved sixty-five dollars on our food. It's not what we buy; it's how we buy it that makes the difference.

As for the question about my time and the driving around, that is inconsequential. If I was driving huge distances for one item that was only a dollar or two less, then yes, that would be a waste. But all of the stores I use (and advise people to use) are within a few miles of where we usually are driving. That means that the gas cost isn't more than three dollars per week, even at high gas prices. The time factor is usually one to two hours per week at the most. If that saves me sixty-five dollars then I am doing great, and it is more than worth it.

So my answer to this question is always the same: Yes, it makes a difference to shop smart. I am always trying to teach my kids this. I often hear, "Oh, Mom, it's only a couple of dollars." Then I shop for them and save ten dollars on two items. It's more than a little bit of money. What if I applied that attitude to twenty-five items—I would save $125. That's another week's worth of groceries—at least!

3. *Is buying the cheapest always the best way to go?*

I love this question. It is the question whose answer divides the cheap from the frugal. Frugal people are looking for the best overall value. That value may not be money. Cheap people always put money first.

I left a high-paying job in order to be a stay-at-home mom. That was not a financially wise move, but it paid off for my family and my children's sake. Whenever we decide to buy or not buy something, we need to make sure the overall choice is best for us. In many cases, the cost can be the deciding factor, but not always.

Doing research on how good the product is that you are buying is the most important thing you can do. Find out if it has a reliable track record. Will it cost you more down the road in repairs or replacements? This goes for anything from small household items to homes and cars. We have friends who got a "great deal" on a fairly new home but later found it plagued with physical defects and deed problems. In the end it cost them more than buying a more expensive home in the first place. We bought a car that had one of those 100,000-mile head-to-toe warranties, thinking we would be gaining in the long run. Little did we know that that manufacturer is notorious for car defects and for not honoring the warranty (finding technicalities to deny it). We would have been better off buying something else.

Whatever you buy, do the math on the end cost to you. Buying used can sometimes be good, but not always. Some items could not only be more expensive to buy used, but could also cause you some health problems that will cost you in more ways than money. There are some items that I will never buy used, such as shoes, humidifiers, and mattresses, just to name a few. Shoes have been molded to the feet of the previous owner and can cause foot, leg, and back problems to another person, as they cause you to walk differently than you normally do. Humidifiers can harbor mold and other elements that can cause you health problems. Mattresses, like shoes, are molded by the sleeper and sag, which can cause back troubles. They also collect bacteria and other things and should be sanitized before buying. This can be done but is an added expense and hassle. Many resale shops are required by state law to have this done before they resell a mattress.

Buying a used car may be the best financial choice for most of us, but make sure you have factored in all of the costs involved. Many people only look at the purchase price and think they will be okay. This is especially important for teens buying their first car. Make sure all other expenses are factored in. Here are some expenses to make sure you can cover:

- The sales tax after you buy it, paid to the Department of Motor Vehicles upon transferring the title (usually about 10 percent of the value of the car)

- Tires (usually annual expense of $100 to $150)

- Car insurance (can be $100 to $300 per month depending on the car and driving record)

- Annual registration of the car with the Department of Motor Vehicles (anywhere from $25 to $350 per year, depending on the state you live in and the car)

- Regular maintenance such as oil changes, tune-ups, etc. (depends on the number of miles you drive, but can be $300 to $1000 per year)

4. *Aren't you depriving your children of important opportunities? Wouldn't they be better off with you working?*

I don't believe the key to a good family or good child rearing lies in having "the right amount" of money. And what is that right amount, anyway? I have seen families with plenty of money have poor family situations. Money is not what defines success.

I don't believe children need all of the things that society says they need. And I've noticed that the list of "needs" for children varies from county to county. When we lived in the San Francisco Bay Area, they "needed" three to four extra-curricular activities per week in order to be considered a well-rounded child. Just going hiking, making crafts, and visiting friends and relatives was considered depriving them. Now that I live in Colorado, the list is less demanding but can still vary from city to city.

Often that list of "needs" is really for the parents' sake and not the child's. The parents want to be able to say that their child is involved in this or that. Their own personal status and sense of success lies in how successful their children appear. So if a child is average or content with just fishing and hiking, the parents panic. What will they talk about at the office cooler if their kids aren't successful?

Another reason parents feel the need to over-provide is to make sure their child is the best at school. They feel the child must never deal with being harassed for not having something: the latest fashion, the latest MP3 player, cars, vacations, etc. Since we are training our children for how to deal with life, that thinking will only train them to define themselves by what they have and how they look instead of who they are inside.

I have had women tell me they would rather go to work and have the kids in child care after school so there is money for extra activities. I wonder how much the kids would prefer for those activities to be with Mom.

By prioritizing our spending and choosing things that provide value and meaning, we still enjoy the beauty of life, family, and well-chosen things. Having more things doesn't give happiness. But well-chosen purchases that might take time to arrange are valued.

For those new to the frugal lifestyle, there might be some adjustments needed. Perhaps you shop recreationally, eat out often, and vacation "in style" by skiing or traveling whenever you want. Learning new ways to find enjoyable activities will take some time, and relearning how to live and shop might be difficult at first. But there's a sense of satisfaction when you see that you have set the values for your family and not allowed society to set them for you. And the best part is no one will be deprived. On the contrary, they will be the fortunate ones, having learned self-discipline, saving, patience, reusing, and ingenuity.

5. *How do we go on vacation with little money? We want to fly somewhere.*

At times we do want to go on a trip that doesn't involve camping or visiting relatives. And there are ways to afford that even on a frugal budget. It usually takes some time and planning, but it can be done.

If you have some time, the most gainful way to save on a trip is to use some sort of rebate credit card. We run our purchases through these cards and pay them off at the end of the month, treating the charges just like a checkbook charge. The points add up quickly and we end up with free airline miles to our destination. This takes some time to accumulate, and then some lead time to book enough free seats on the flights. For our lodging, we look for places with kitchens or microwaves and refrigerators so we can save on cooking in instead of eating out. We usually look for condos on Web sites where owners post them for rent, and avoid any agencies.

When we haven't had the time to accumulate the miles and book seats in advance, we have found some good airline and hotel deals online. There are several travel Web sites that search all of the other travel Web sites, making it the most comprehensive search around. Our favorite search engine for travel deals is *www.Kayak.com*. It covers hotels and cars as well, but we find we can do better on those elsewhere, and we use Kayak mainly for airfare deals. The best hotel deals we have found are at *www.hotwire.com*, but it comes with a quirk. You can pick the location and how many stars the hotel has, but the actual name of the hotel remains a mystery until you pay. We find good car deals at *www.carrentals.com* or at Hotwire.

At times a road trip costs us less than flying. To make that economical, we look for any hotel chains that are offering deals if we stay at their hotels along the way. We found one chain that offered free breakfasts, kitchenettes in the room, and a rebate if we use them for all of our night stays along the way. We used this plan when we drove to the Grand Canyon. To save on food, we kept a cooler in the car that we refilled at grocery stores. This was much cheaper than eating fast food. For savings on gasoline, we used a gas rebate credit card. One year we even rented a more gas-economical car than the one we owned. The gas savings was more than the rental fee.

During the leanest of years, we have enjoyed vacations at home. Exploring the tourist attractions at home, picnics, hikes, and more can be very refreshing and economical when needed.

Menu Plans

Using the following menus, it is possible to feed a family of four for about $65 per week. All of these meals are what we eat. They are frugal if made from scratch. Repeat some meals if you can. Many more will be featured in my cookbook, *Healthy Meals For Less*. (Some of the recipes for these meals can be found within this book.)

Breakfast
>Homemade granola
>Homemade cinnamon rolls
>Muffins
>Hot cereal (oatmeal or cream of wheat)
>Pancakes, French toast, or waffles with homemade pan-cake syrup

Lunches
>Peanut butter and jelly sandwiches
>Chicken salad sandwiches (made with leftover chicken)
>Lunch-meat sandwiches
>Hot dogs
>Tuna sandwiches
>Cheese and crackers
>Macaroni and cheese
>Soup and crackers

Homemade burgers
Bagels and cream cheese
Leftovers

Snacks & Fruits
Homemade cookies and granola bars
Homemade banana bread
Popcorn (caramel, spiced, plain)
Rice pudding
Salads
Fresh vegetables
Homemade fruit leather

Drinks
Juices, milk, or water

Dinners
Thai noodle meal
Spaghetti with meatballs
Vegetarian spaghetti (grated vegetables instead of meat)
Chicken and potatoes with cream of mushroom soup
Beans and rice
Fajitas
Homemade veggie burgers
Minestrone soup
Enchilada casserole (tortillas, beans, cheese, and enchilada
    sauce)
Potpies
Stir-fry (using leftover meat)
Burritos
Lentil rice casserole
Quiche
Vegetable patties
Leftover bread dinner

Leek and potato soup
Anne's squash casserole
Black bean soup
Huevos rancheros
Leftover chicken Italian meal
Leftovers smorgasbord
Baked potato smorgasbord
Vegetarian chili and homemade cornbread
Easy microwave lasagna
Messy chicken
Indian curry
Chinese pineapple chicken
Pizza
Poor-man's steak

Additional Resources

Here are some very good resources for learning more about how to live on less. Some chapters have their own resource section with applicable books. These are in addition to those.

MISERLY LIVING

Brennen, Sherri. *Better Living: Tips for Saving Time and Money.* WVEC-TV Inc., 1994.

Dacyczyn, Amy. *The Complete Tightwad Gazette: Promoting Thrift as a Viable Alternative Lifestyle.* Villard Books, 1999.

Dappen, Andy. *Cheap Tricks: 100s of Ways You Can Save 1000s of Dollars.* Brier Books, 1992.

Editors of Rodale. *Cut Your Spending in Half Without Settling for Less.* Rodale Press, 1995.

Ellis, Gwen, and Jo Ann Janssen. *Decorating on a Shoestring.* Broadman Holman, 1999.

Gallagher, Patricia. *Raising Happy Kids on a Reasonable Budget.* Better Way Books, 1993.

Gorman, Charlotte. *The Frugal Mind: 1,483 Money-Saving Tips for Surviving the New Millennium.* Nottingham Books, 1998.

Hunt, Mary. *The Best of the Cheapskate Monthly: Simple Tips for Living Lean in the '90s.* St. Martin's Paperbacks, 1993.

Lesko, Matthew. *Free Stuff for Busy Moms.* Information USA, Inc., 1999.

McBride, Tracey. *Frugal Luxuries: Simple Pleasures to Enhance Your Life and Comfort Your Soul.* Bantam Books, 1997.

McCoy, Jonni. *Frugal Families: Making the Most of Your Hard-Earned Money.* Full Quart Press, 1998.

Miller, Mark W. *The Complete Idiot's Guide to Being a Cheapskate.* Macmillan, 1998.

Moore, Melodie. *The Frugal Almanac: Over 500 Money-Saving Ideas.* NAL, 1997.

Paris, James L. *Absolutely Amazing Ways to Save Money on Everything.* Harvest House, 1999.

Roberts, William. *How to Save Money on Just About Everything.* Paladin Press, 1996.

Roth, Larry. *The Best of Living Cheap News: Practical Advice on Saving Money and Living Well.* NTC Publishing Group, 1996.

Simmons, Lee, and Barbara Simmons. *Penny-Pinching: How to Lower Your Everyday Expenses Without Lowering Your Standard of Living.* Bantam Books, 1999.

Taylor-Hough, Deborah. *A Simple Choice: A Practical Guide for Saving Your Time, Money, and Sanity.* Champion Books, 2000.

Yates, Cynthia. *The Complete Guide to Creative Gift Giving.* Servant Publications, 1997.

Yorkey, Mike. *21 Days to a Thrifty Lifestyle.* Zondervan, 1997.

FAMILY BUDGETING AND SAVINGS

Briles, Judith. *10 Smart Money Moves for Women: How to Conquer Your Financial Fears.* NTC, 1999.

Burkett, Larry. *Your Complete Guide to Financial Security*. Budget Book Service, 1998.

Chilton, David. *The Wealthy Barber: Everyone's Commonsense Guide to Becoming Financially Independent.* Prima Publishing, 1998.

Detweiler, Gerri, Marc Eisenson, and Nancy Castleman. *Invest in Yourself: Six Secrets to a Rich Life.* John Wiley & Sons, 1998.

Humber, Wilson J. *Dollars and Sense: Making the Most of What You Have.* Navpress, 1993.

O'Neill, Barbara. *Saving on a Shoestring: How to Cut Expenses, Reduce Debt, Stash More Cash.* Dearborn Financial Publishing, Inc., 1995.

Pond, Jonathan. *The New Century Family Money Book.* Dell Hardcover, 1993.

Savage, Terry. *Terry Savage's New Money: Strategies for the '90s.* Harper Business, 1994.

Scott, David. *The Guide to Personal Budgeting: How to Stretch Your Dollars Through Wise Money Management.* Globe Pequot, 1995.

Wall, Ginita. *The Way to Save: A 10-Step Blueprint for Lifetime Security.* Henry Holt and Co., 1993.

GETTING OUT OF DEBT AND BEING FINANCIALLY FREE

Blue, Ron. *Taming the Money Monster: Five Steps to Conquering Debt.* Focus on the Family Publishing, 1993.

Brunette, William K. *Conquer Your Debt.* Prentice Hall Press, 1990.

Detweiler, Gerri, Marc Eisenson, and Nancy Castleman. *Slash Your Debt*. Financial Literacy Center, 1999.

Hunt, Mary. *The Cheapskate Monthly Money Makeover*. St. Martin's Paperbacks, 1995.

Paris, James L. *Living Financially Free*. Harvest House Publishers, 1994.

STARTING A HOME BUSINESS

Brabec, Barbara. *Homemade Money—How to Select, Start, Manage, Market and Multiply the Profits of a Business at Home*. Better Way Books, 1997.

Demas, Cheryl. *The Work-at-Home Mom's Guide to Home Business: Stay at Home and Make Money With Wahm.Com*. Hazen Publishers, Inc., 2000.

Folger, Liz. *The Stay-at-Home Mom's Guide to Making Money: How to Create the Business That's Right for You, Using the Skills and Interests You Already Have*. Prima Publishing, 2000.

Gwen, Ellis. *101 Ways to Make Money at Home*. Vine Books, 1996.

Huff, Priscilla Y. *101 Best Home-Based Businesses for Women*. Prima Publishing, 1998.

Hull, Caroline, and Tanya Wallace. *Moneymaking Moms: How Work at Home Can Work for You*. Citadel Press, 1998.

Levinson, Jay. *555 Ways to Earn Extra Money*. Henry Holt, 1991.

Oberlin, Loriann H. *Working at Home While the Kids Are There Too*. Career Press, 1997.

Parlapiano, Ellen H. *Mompreneurs: A Mother's Practical Step-by-Step Guide to Work-at-Home Success*. Berkley Publishing Group, 1996.

Partow, Donna. *Homemade Business: A Woman's Step-by-Step*

Guide to Earning Money at Home. Focus on the Family Publishing, 1999.

Roberts, Lisa M. *How to Raise a Family and a Career Under One Roof: A Parent's Guide to Home Business.* Bookhaven Press, 1997.

Sanders, Darcie, and Martha Bullen. *Turn Your Talents Into Profits: 100+ Terrific Ideas for Starting Your Own Home-Based Microbusiness.* Simon & Schuster, 1998.

Books by
Jonni McCoy
<small>FROM BETHANY HOUSE PUBLISHERS</small>

Healthy Meals for Less
Miserly Moms